Associated Press

Guide to Photojournalism

Second Edition

Brian Horton

McGraw-Hill

New York San Francisco Washington, D.C. Auckland Bogota
Caracas Lisbon London Madrid Mexico City Milan
Montreal New Delhi San Juan Singapore
Sydney Tokyo Toronto

This book is dedicated to Fred Wright, Jack Schwadel, Tom diLustro, Bill Ingraham and the thousands of other photographers and photo editors who have inspired us. There is so much we can learn including one key lesson: content is what counts.

Crash of the Hindenburg.
Murray Becker, Lakehurst, N.J., 1937

Post-war portrait.
Michael Nash, Warsaw, 1946

Willie Mays makes spring training catch.
Uncredited, Phoenix, 1956

Contents

McGraw-Hill
A Division of The McGraw-Hill Companies

ISBN: 0-07-136387-4

McGraw-Hill books are available at special quantity discounts to use as premiums and sales promotions, or for use in corporate training programs. For more information, please write to the Director of Special Sales, McGraw-Hill, 2 Penn Plaza, New York, NY 10121. Or contact your local bookstore.

Book design by Loren Fisher
Layout by Elf Multimedia, www.ElfMultimedia.com

7890BAN/BAN098

Other Titles in The Associated Press Series
Associated Press Broadcast News Handbook

Foreword

Information seekers demanding to "see" what others write about has made the role of pictures vital in the world's information flow of the 21st century. Driven by this need, the use of pictures as information is changing — more pictures are dramatically used, there is greater reliance on visual devices to tell stories and provide insight.

This new, intense use of the visual boils down to photography. And that is what this book, the *Associated Press Guide to Photojournalism*, is all about.

The author, Brian Horton, has a unique background for this volume. He is educated in journalism; he has worked as a photographer and has covered virtually every kind of story news people encounter; he has been a picture editor. In the latter capacity he has planned the work of photography and reviewed the work of photographers. He is young enough to recognize the good in the new, and old enough to save the best of the past.

This book is not a manual. Much has been written elsewhere about the technology of photography, how to operate a camera, how to judge exposure, how to crop pictures and plan a printed page or a dot-com screen.

This book is about the essence of photography, about the editor and photographer's minds at work seeking the most elusive of all journalistic ends, a fine picture that tells those who see it something about their world.

To put it another way, this book is about content. I assure you, as a journalist who has coped with the challenges of technology and content, that content is more difficult.

The precious skill — "seeing the story" and therefore providing meaningful content — is developed in a variety of ways. It requires education, experience, desire, knowledge, insight and that rarest factor of all, talent. And using all those factors in one instant to provide a picture that tells us more then we knew before.

It takes a lifetime to learn to do that. No one ever masters it completely because there is always a bit of serendipity in every new situation the picture journalist faces. What this book does is take you into the minds of photographers who have dealt with a broad spectrum of assignments. The best of them will tell you that the old adage is true: Chance favors the prepared mind.

To help the picture journalist meet the challenge of preparation, the *Associated Press Guide to Photojournalism* creates an opportunity few other books on photography offer. Horton, through his interviews, gives the reader the benefit of the years of experience, the hours and days of preparation, the grasp of insight and other skills fine photographers bring to each assignment.

You will walk with photographers in Vietnam; chase a tornado with another cameraman; learn about the tedium of hours and days of waiting for the great picture that then comes in a cat's wink of time; you will move through the human debris of an air crash.

Horton also offers the picture journalist a look at digital photography, both the good and the not so good aspects of film-less photos, and the challenge this technology brings to content and to credibility.

In short, the careful reader of the *Associated Press Guide to Photojournalism* will have the opportunity to share the telescoped experience and talents of others who have done the job well and are willing to share their knowledge.

Hal Buell
AP Photo Editor (retired)

About the Author

Brian Horton, Associated Press senior photo editor for sports, is a 29-year veteran of the news cooperative.

His coverage resume, as a photographer and photo editor, includes the World Series, the Super Bowl, horse racing's Triple Crown, the Winter and Summer Olympics since 1984, World Cup soccer, the Indianapolis 500, the major golf tournaments, the Final Four, the NBA Finals and many other large sports events.

He also has covered news events ranging from the Persian Gulf War in Saudi Arabia and Kuwait to coal mine disasters, presidential campaigns and political conventions.

Horton grew up in Indiana and attended Indiana University before joining the AP in Chicago in 1971 as a photo editor. He later had assignments as a staff photographer in Philadelphia and Cincinnati, was Ohio NewsPhoto Editor based in Columbus and transferred to New York in 1982 as Photo Enterprise Editor. Horton was named LaserPhoto Network Director in 1987 and was named Senior Photo Editor for Sports in 1992.

In addition to his photo editing duties, Horton has lectured here and abroad on topics including color photo usage and reproduction, informational graphics and photojournalism.

In 1986, Horton was honored by the National Press Photographers Association for his manual on improving color usage and also for the workshops he conducted on the topic. Horton is the author of an AP book, *The Picture,* the predecessor to this edition, published in 1989, which was extensively used as a text for college and young professional photographers. With his wife, Marilyn Dillon, he was the picture editor for another AP book, *Moments in Sports,* a compilation of noted sports photos from the AP's archive.

In 2000, Horton was named winner of the Gramling Achievement Award, given for his significant contributions to the news report and the overall success of the AP.

Horton and his wife live in suburban New Jersey.

From the Author

This book has been an education for me.

With a phone pressed to my ear as I made notes, I've listened to hours of wonderful, horrible, inspirational and thoughtful moments related by the photographers, photo editors, educators and journalists who are the contributors to this book.

The stories they have told, the insights they have offered, the lessons they have shared have made me proud to be part of the fraternity of photojournalists.

It has been an honor to be allowed inside their thought processes. To hear how they handled various situations. To hear about their triumphs and their failures. To marvel at how open they would all be to helping other photojournalists get a step ahead in this business we are part of.

More than ten years ago, I wrote the first edition of this book. At the time, I expressed the hope that the book would provide the basic building blocks for a photojournalist. I didn't promise suggestions on which lens to use, or what shutter speed to set a camera, but I did promise the book would provide a peek behind the scenes. The thought process of photography, as it were.

Since that first book came out, I have gotten dozens of letters from students, young professionals, teachers and even a few more-seasoned professionals, and met photographers on assignments, who have read the book. They have been kind in their praise and compliments and one even told me he had inspirational quotes from the book on the wall of his darkroom.

But it was the contributors to that book and to this new edition who deserve the praise. They had lived it and were willing to share.

A book like this doesn't come together in a vacuum. Obviously, the people quoted gave so much of their time. But, even more, there were people behind the scenes who gave so willingly, too.

My wife, Marilyn Dillon, offered suggestions and encouragement during the formative stages which made the book a lot better than it would have been. Her input is stamped throughout. For that, a simple thanks isn't enough.

Chuck Zoeller of the AP's photo library pulled my bacon out of the fire more than once. Suggestions on content and help in tracking down an errant image or two were among the things he did.

The AP's Sports Photo Desk crew (Paul Kazdan, Melissa Einberg, Tracy Gitnick and Dan Derella) covered for me while I had my head in the book and never let a thing drop through the cracks. For their vigilance, my thanks.

Finally, I'd like to thank Hal Buell, my mentor, an inspiration, and a source for all things journalistic for so many years. He's the person who pushed American newspapers into the digital age, the person who is the walking history lesson of photojournalism in the latter stages of the 20th century. And, a dear friend who never says no when you need someone to talk with. For all of that, thanks.

And, to all of my AP colleagues, and the photojournalists I've met and worked with from newspapers and magazines over the years, a thank you for allowing me to share a bench with you on the front row of history.

Brian Horton
Long Beach Island, N.J.
2000

Introduction

It can be a picture of a trio of men fighting the elements as hurricane-whipped waves wash a home into the ocean. The fury of the storm captured in a picture by a photographer who isn't afraid to get wet doing his job.

It can be a picture of a tiny youngster playfully trying to push back his hulking opponent, a Sumo wrestler. Not an earth-shaking moment of history, but a fun picture that makes you smile.

It can be a picture of hundreds of flash bulbs going off at once as fans try to capture slugger Mark McGwire hitting a record home run. Thinking on the part of the photojournalist of a different way to tell a story.

It can be a picture, an instant recording, of a heavily armed government agent reaching for young Cuban immigrant Elian Gonzalez. The photo would elicit emotional responses from people on both sides of the political issue and fuel heated discussions about the government intervention, too.

It can be a picture, a portrait really, of a young boy with a small bunch of flowers in his hand on his way to pay his respects to Mother Teresa. His eyes lock on to the viewer of the photo.

It can be a picture of a lone bagpiper leaving his footsteps in the dew as he strides into the mists after an emotional memorial service for a popular golfer who has died tragically. The viewer can't help but feel the sadness of the moment.

Opposite page: David Longstreath, Calcutta, 1997

Alan Diaz, Miami, 2000 (top); Amy Sancetta, Leominster, Mass., 1998 (above left); Paul Sakuma, San Jose, Calif., 1993 (right)

Pat Sullivan, Houston, 1999 (left); Dave Martin, Key West, Fla., 1998 (below right); Ed Reinke, St. Louis, 1998 (bottom)

It can be a picture, a portrait of sorts, of the inventor of the pink flamingo surrounded by his wares. A slice of Americana.

It's all photojournalism.

Telling a story with a picture, reporting with a camera, recording a moment in time, the fleeting instant when an image sums up a story. Henri Cartier-Bresson called it the "decisive moment."

Happiness, sadness, accomplishment, failure, relief, fear, death -- the mosaic of our lives captured on film and on electronic disks.

Photojournalism isn't just a spot news picture made in a war in an exotic location far away. Datelines don't change the quality of a picture. It's also the local city council meeting, or state legislature, where members are arguing about a tax increase or a new law.

It's not just a national magazine cover picture showing the key play from the Super Bowl. It's also the local high school team, anywhere in America, playing for the town's glory.

It's not just an essay on rafting down the Mekong River in Asia. It's also people keeping cool under a water spray on a hot day in your town.

Photographers covering the president of the United States or the mayor of a small town have the same mission -- to make an accurate reporting of the subject's activities.

Photographers covering the Oklahoma City bombing, which struck at the heart of America in the worst domestic terrorism case in its history, or a smoky house fire that displaces a family, have the same mission -- to convey the enormity of the event in human terms.

Photographers covering the last out of the World Series or the last seconds of a high school basketball game have the same mission -- to capture the essence of the winner's happiness, and the lonely moments and despair of the losers.

Moments that are part of our history -- big and small.

In each case, venues may be different, but the mission is the same -- to inform, to report, to carry the scene to the readers, whether they are thousands of miles away or just down the street. To show them something they might not have had a chance to see themselves. To grab a moment of history and preserve it for the future.

Most agree it takes a special kind of passion for photojournalism to be successful. Passion that elevates one photographer above another.

"Technical ability aside, the difference is commitment," says Western Kentucky University photojournalism program director Mike Morse. "Some people look at whatever they do as a job and they want to be good craftsmen. Then there are people who do it as a passion. They really care about it, and it shows in their photographs."

J. Bruce Baumann, the managing editor

> It takes a special kind of passion for photojournalism to be successful. Passion that elevates one photographer above another.

of *The Courier and Press* in Evansville, Ind., says it is important for the photojournalist to think first as a journalist, second as a photographer.

Baumann believes photographers need to reach out more for excellence these days. "It seems to me that the real guts of journalism, the reason I got in this business, is to make a difference," he says, "to present the lives of people, their joys, their fears, their happiness and sadness. To tell the world what is going on around them."

Baumann says photographers should be "looking for new ideas, new themes, breaking new ground, looking for things that are happening."

From Matthew Brady's coverage of the Civil War to the social reporting of Lewis Hine and Jacob Riis at the turn of the century, from the documentary photography of Walker Evans and Dorothea Lange in the 1930s to the Life magazine photojournalists W. Eugene Smith and Alfred Eisenstaedt and today's avant-garde images of David LaChapelle and Nick Knight, there is a fine heritage of photography to look at and study.

There are lessons to be learned from

photographers who pioneered the photographic styles used today by countless newspaper and magazine photographers. And lessons to be learned by making pictures yourself.

Several years ago, a newspaper group ran an ad showing a photographer in combat gear. The caption: "Be prepared for a few cold dinners." That's certainly true for a photojournalist covering a war, but also true for a photographer covering the local scene.

AP photographer Mark Humphrey looked for more than a news conference to illustrate the continuing story of a state legislative budget impasse in Nashville. His photo of two legislators meeting privately in a hallway is a good illustration of how deals are made in state politics.

Long days are the rule, with the stress of a hundred decisions a part of the everyday life. Will I be in the right place? Will I make the picture I want? Will I select the right lens and exposure to tell the story? When the moment comes, will everything I've learned give me the tools to make the picture that will tell the story of the event I'm covering?

Associated Press photographer Amy Sancetta explains: "You have to love this job because the schedules, the emotional ups and downs, the pressures would sometimes be too much if you didn't love it. It's a creative field. If you go to a game and make a good picture or shoot a nice por-

A Kenyan woman weeps during a memorial service for victims of the 1998 terrorist bombing of the U.S. embassy in Nairobi. Photographer Jean-Marc Bouju, on assignment for the AP, used a wide angle lens and filled the frame.

trait, you go home feeling great, but if you miss something, you go home feeling awful."

J. Pat Carter likens it to the tightrope walker in the circus. "Everyone is waiting for you to fall, but when you make it across, they yell, 'Bravo. Encore,' and they applaud." Every photographer lives for that applause, those "bravos!," the Oklahoma City-based AP photographer says.

The burden of the news you cover can be a heavy load.

"With that camera," Carter says, "you are the eyes of your readers and your viewers and you have to take them there. Sometimes I am uncomfortable but I have a job to do. If you don't feel uncomfortable at

times, if you don't share in the emotion, you are not going to have the heart and soul to do the job anyway.

"You can't be the tough guy all the time. You can't be the guy who doesn't cry," he says.

Laura Rauch, an AP photographer based in Las Vegas, was called on to help cover the Columbine High School shootings near Denver. Then she returned there a year later to assist in coverage of the first anniversary.

Both times, there was an emotional toll.

Rauch's family was from the area, so there was some family history, some familiarity, to figure in the equation. But this was bigger than that. "I don't think you had to have family from that area for it to hurt," she says. "I don't care who you are. That one is going to hurt, because it is such a tragedy."

Covering the initial story and then the follow-up exposed Rauch to scenes of tremendous grief and sadness. "High school kids," she says, "who had lost their friends in what is supposed to be the most carefree time of their lives. Many, many photographers, including me, were overcome with the sadness of it all.

A 15-year-old high school student leans on her mother during a candlelight vigil in Littleton, Colo., marking the one-year anniversary of the 1999 shooting deaths at Columbine High School. "Many, many photographers, including me, were overcome with the sadness of it all," says AP photographer Laura Rauch.

"I would have to take a moment and cry a little. I would let it go for a minute, and then I'd suck it up and start shooting again," she says.

Ed Reinke, an AP photographer, recalls a bus crash that killed more than two dozen teen-agers on their way home from an amusement park. After days of covering the emotional scenes at cemeteries, churches and funeral homes, "I had come to the end of my line on what I could take."

Reinke's answer after the story wound down was to "take a few days off and hold my own kids and think about how fortunate I am."

Years later, Reinke would be in Japan covering an Olympics, when he got word his wife and two sons had been injured in a head-on crash so violent that it totaled the family car. He was moved to tears as he thought of being on the other side of the world, on an assignment considered to be a bright point in his career, when his family needed him.

The cost of that kind of commitment to the job can't be measured.

Once, after going five weeks without fresh water while covering the conflict in Sarajevo, Paris AP staffer Jerome Delay called home to find out that the family washing machine was broken. It took him a moment, he says, to realize that to his family this was a serious situation. "Even though it might not be important to you at the time," he says, "it is important to them, and you have to respect that and show your concern."

David Longstreath, also an AP staffer, calls it a balancing act -- the professional

And, that means keeping in touch with your feelings and the feelings of the people you are photographing.

"Once you pull those cameras out," he says, "you're involved. You have to bear the weight of the comments and stares. You try to do it with a degree of sensitivity." The balance, he says, is to "be sensitive to their needs, but still do the job."

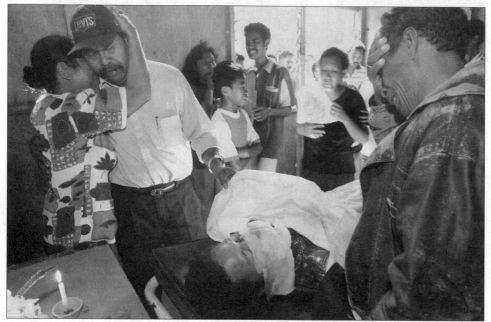

A family grieves over the body of their slain son in a makeshift morgue in Dili, East Timor. He died in a 1999 gun battle in the fight for independence there. AP photographer David Longstreath spent the day with the family as they identified the body, then took it home for burial. For the assignment, he said he had to be "sensitive to their needs, but still do the job."

Michel DuCille of the *Washington Post* says any photographer's approach should be about "treating subjects with dignity and losing your preconceived notions. Be a strong anticipator of human nature and be in the right place at the right time."

responsibilities and the personal turmoil.

Longstreath covered the Oklahoma City federal building bombing while based in that city. He was at the scene minutes after the explosion crushed the building. He was exposed to a horrific scene.

"One of the things that I learned after the Oklahoma City bombing," he says, "is that every situation is going to impact you and you have to just recognize that you are a human. You may put your feelings on hold while you finish the job, but at some point you have to allow yourself to feel, as well."

Delay says you need to not only know when and where to make pictures, but just as important, you need to be sensitive to when you should pull away.

"There are times when I say to myself, 'Leave these people alone,' but there is no rule," Delay says. He draws frequent assignments to tumultuous situations in the Balkans and other hot spots where people often are on the edge emotionally.

"You just know when it is right to go," he says. "You feel it. As you get older, the more experience you have, the fewer wrong calls you make. You can see when you are being intrusive. It's a little like dancing with wolves."

AP photographer Elise Amendola says sometimes you have to draw from your emotional reservoir when you are dealing with a sensitive situation. "I think an important time to draw upon the emotional reservoir is during a one-on-one with someone who has lost a loved one in an accident, illness or war," she says.

"It's a frequent assignment," says Amendola, describing a recent assignment where she photographed a woman who had lost her daughter in a teen car wreck. "It helped me to empathize with her. And I mean with genuine patience, eye contact and real conversation. Too often, we're in a rush. But in these instances, it's a must to take the time to establish rapport and a trust. This is when the ability to empathize puts

heart into your photography." Amendola says if you're rushed or uninterested, "it just doesn't work. And that shows in your pictures."

"When I started out," Rauch says, "I

The effects of flash flooding after a storm in 1999 were captured by AP photographer Laura Rauch in her photo of an 85-year-old man in the yard of his Las Vegas home. Rauch thinks the role of the photojournalist is important, "but it is never more important than the people you photograph, ever."

thought the role of the photojournalist was the most important thing in the world." The years have tempered those feelings a bit for her. "It is important," she says, "but it is never more important than the people you photograph, ever."

Thought, planning and a good chunk of luck cut down the chances for failure, but photographers have to be prepared, whether on the biggest assignment of their career, or the pet of the week at the animal shelter, to bring back the picture that really tells the story to the reader.

Reinke says it is the art of being able to go with the flow, with some control. He explains, "I think it becomes a thinking

Longstreath describes that "flow" management another way. At a news scene, he says, "you throw your antenna out, you look, and you size it up. Pretty soon you see your opening, and you're in."

Faced with a dramatic rescue during flooding after Hurricane Hortense hit Puerto Rico in 1996, AP photographer John McConnico sized up the scene and selected the right lens to capture the drama from the edge of the swollen stream.

"If you are not prepared when opportunity knocks," says J. Scott Applewhite of the AP's Washington bureau, "you'll only be left complaining about the noise."

Or, as famed Green Bay Packers football coach Vince Lombardi used to tell his players, "Luck, that's where preparation meets opportunity."

Great photographers come from a variety of backgrounds. As children, many began making pictures with a simple box camera, developing the film in crude darkrooms set up in the family's bathroom. They watched the contact prints develop in little trays balanced on the edge of the sink, while family members waited impatiently to use the facilities.

person's game. Anyone can stick a camera in the face of the obvious, but a truly good photojournalist will look at the situation and the light that is there, and the light you are carrying in your bag, and the cameras and lenses you have, and make the best possible picture out of what you have."

"That is what separates a good photographer from a mediocre one, " Reinke says, "the ability to go with the flow, but also to have a general idea of how the flow goes."

For Kansas City AP staffer Cliff Schiappa, it was a different inconvenience for his family members. Schiappa got a job making pictures for the local weekly before he got his driver's license. So, his mom and dad would drive him to his assignments and wait patiently in the car while he made his pictures.

AP photographer Harry Cabluck began his photo career in high school when he raced to auto accidents, alerted by the dispatcher at his family's towing business, in hopes of making a picture. Then he'd try for a sale to the local newspaper or, perhaps, an insurance company. On weekend nights, he'd troop up and down the sidelines of high school football games, making flash exposures powered by a homemade car battery setup.

Sports Illustrated photographer John Biever also got his start covering football games, but at a slightly higher level. At the age of 14, he was working the sidelines with his dad, Green Bay Packers team photographer Vernon Biever, and even got a doubletruck spread in Look magazine that first season with a photo of famed Packers

quarterback Bart Starr.

AP's Bob Daugherty got his start on the high school newspaper and yearbook in Marion, Ind. But, at the tender age of 15, he moved to a full-time spot on the local

During a 1992 debate between presidential candidates, photographer Marcy Nighswander, then with the AP, chose a position away from the other photographers. The result was this photo, part of the AP's Pulitzer Prize winning entry on the '92 campaign.

newspaper's staff. Before long, he was working at the state's largest paper.

To learn about photography, Daugherty had studied the Indianapolis newspapers. One of the photographers was an expert in shooting in available-light situations, two others "could do wonders with a single light." Later, he would work beside many of the photographers he had studied so carefully when starting out.

Others, like Reinke, took up the profession after getting a camera as a high school graduation gift, asking friends for help in the basics of loading the camera and adjusting the aperture and shutter speeds. He credits his college photojournalism professor, Dr. Will Counts of Indiana University, for his direct, honest approach to photography.

He says of his visual style: "The single thing that influenced me was 'Self Portrait: USA,' a book by David Douglas Duncan." Reinke says that book, a collection of Duncan's photographs from the tumultuous 1968 political conventions in Chicago and Miami, opened his eyes to a way of making pictures that he still aspires to today.

AP photographer Mark Duncan went to college and drove an oil delivery truck for his family's business, making pictures in his spare time before moving into his first full-time staff job in the photo department of the *Dayton Daily News.*

"Go to college and get a degree in photojournalism," he tells prospective photographers, "and have the opportunity to have internships." Duncan studied computer science in college. "I am grateful for my computer background because of where the industry is going, but more journalism would have balanced that. The journalism part is important. My job is not just to take pictures, but to impart information."

Some photographers, like Longstreath, learned the fine points of their craft in the military, starting with basic documentation tasks and advancing to elite camera groups and advanced studies. From a high school photo course, to a job as a "lab rat" for the FBI, he went on to the Navy and more formal training, before leaving the service and moving into daily photojournalism.

Photographer Mark Duncan drove a fuel-oil delivery truck for his family's business and worked part time making pictures before joining the Dayton Daily News. Now with the AP and based in Cleveland, Duncan's daily assignments include coverage like this 1999 WNBA game.

The military gave him great training and a chance to work with some excellent photographers, but, "after assignments in thirty-three countries, I had personally witnessed too many pier-side goodbyes," Longstreath said.

Des Moines Register director of photography John Gaps III got into photography after being the subject during his days as a prep football player. Gaps tells the story: "A photographer showed me some pictures that he had made of me playing football in high school. Later, I went to his darkroom and I thought

AP's David Longstreath got his first taste of photography in high school, then on to advanced photo assignments in the military before joining the AP. His assignments have taken him all over the world, including Vietnam and that country's 2000 celebration marking the end of its civil war.

that was pretty neat. And then one afternoon in college, I had a choice of going to football practice or finishing a project due in my photography class."

"I gave up football for photography," Gaps says, laughing, "and the coach was real supportive." Gaps explains he wasn't NFL material on the football field. He did, however, get to the Super Bowl several times in his career. With his cameras. And, Gaps now has numerous regional and national awards, and top assignments, to

his credit for his photography.

Rusty Kennedy, an AP photographer, says working everyday with the veteran photographers at his first job, an internship on the photo staff of the former Philadelphia Bulletin, was really his education. "I was really lucky to have learned from them. Each had an area of expertise. One was good at fashion, one was good at studio, and so on. I could watch and learn so much, then try it myself."

Kennedy says you can only get so much from a book or watching, though. "Photography is really such a hands-on thing that you have to do it yourself," he says.

Longstreath believes you learn from everything you see, and you try to keep on learning. "You learn by looking at pictures, by asking how did they do that? You store it away for another day." He, too, feels you learn a lot by simply making pictures. "What worked once may work again with a new twist."

And, you need to be critical of your

tion. "You're as good as you are today," he says. "Then you have to do it again tomorrow."

The common thread that keeps these photographers in the business is the joy of seeing negatives on their film for the first

time -- and after subsequent assignments -- or the print coming up in the developing tray. Or, to screen the slides they've shot and see the impact that they had hoped for. And, now, in the digital age, to call up a disk from a difficult shoot and see the pictures on a computer screen.

Rushing currents and the danger of hitting cars and trucks submerged on the flooded streets of Bound Brook, N.J., made it difficult for AP staffer Dan Hulshizer to maneuver in a small boat as he photographed a fireman checking out a building fire after Hurricane Floyd in 1999.

work. "The minute you are satisfied with the way things look," Longstreath says, "that's the time to quit. You should be constantly striving to improve yourself and your craft."

"There is no such thing as good enough," Longstreath says.

AP photo editor Horst Faas says it is a never-ending reach for better communica-

Daugherty says he thought photography was for him when "I saw my first print come up under the yellow safelight in that tray of Dektol. Then, when I saw the first run of the newspaper," he says, he was hooked for sure. He can't remember that first picture, but laughs and says, "I'm sure it was the best picture I ever made."

After you've worked as a photographer, where do you go? That's changing as photographers become more and more a part of the fabric of the newsroom.

Ten years ago, Baumann wasn't optimistic about the upward mobility for photographers. "There is, for no practical purpose in this country, any place for a photographer to go beyond being an assistant managing editor for photography or graphics," he said at the time.

But now, he says, that isn't as true. Baumann himself, and several other people from the photo ranks, are leading newsrooms across the country.

Ohio University School of Visual Communication director Larry Nighswander says for

Rather than settle for a picture of Microsoft founder Bill Gates at a news conference rostrum, AP photographer Gary Stewart paid attention even after the lights were turned down for a video presentation in 1995. The result was a picture that is still used years later.

readers and to writers."

Efforts to push the envelope of composition and creativity may be diminished if you aren't able to explain your actions. "It may be lost," he says, "to someone who doesn't see the way you see. But if you are

photographers to continue that move into the upper ranks of the decision makers at papers they need to be able to communicate better with their colleagues.

"There is a need," Nighswander says, "for photographers and picture editors to develop a language. The ability to articulate the language of photography. They need to be able to talk to, and about, their photographs to editors and, in some cases, to

able to articulate what it is you are doing and why you are doing it, then you have a better chance of educating others into appreciating the content and the composition."

That kind of communication leads to more respect in the newsroom and that leads to moving up the ladder, several editors say.

"Always make your arguments in the

same terms as if you were making an argument for a story," says newspaper graphics consultant Bob Lynn, who revitalized *The Virginian-Pilot* in Norfolk, Va., while director of photography there.

"If you use the same words they would use to argue for a story, then the word editors can understand what you are trying to say. But," Lynn warns, laughing, "if you use terms like 'visual impact,' you are dead in the water."

People like Baumann and others who have had success, are the ones who could communicate well. "They just didn't say we need to run this picture big," Nighswander says. "They related words and pictures in a way that was all about storytelling. They wanted to make sure words and pictures were working together well so the reader was getting a better package of information."

"Once that was established," Nighswander says, "a smart editor or a smart publisher saw the value of having someone who could elevate both sides of the business."

Lynn also thinks smart picture editors can take advantage of their broader knowledge of the newsroom. A picture editor, Lynn says, routinely works with every section of the paper and also with the production elements. No one else in the newsroom, he says, crosses that spectrum so completely. "As a picture editor, you have to be the best journalist in the newsroom."

Hal Buell, the retired head of the AP's photo operation, says newsroom leaders should be judged on their abilities as journalists, not whether they are good writers or good photo people.

And Buell thinks that only recently have photo people been in a position where they would be considered.

A person, Buell says, "should be put in charge of a newsroom because he or she is a good journalist and understands the many pieces of work that go into making that thing called a newspaper. That includes good writing. It includes good editing. It includes good photography. It includes good headlines and good design."

"The editor in charge of a newsroom needs to be able to see all of those pieces. What has happened historically is that photos was not part of that process," Buell says. Photographers were thought of as mechanics or technicians. Only in recent times has that begun to change with photographers being considered journalists. I think that movement of photo people into the newsroom offers a new dimension to photography in the newspaper."

But, Buell warns, those editors should not favor photographs just as editors who have come through the word ranks should not favor words. "They should be put in charge because they have a sense of what good journalism is and that would include photography."

Photographers have a long heritage of communicating with an image. Most feel passionately about it and take great pride in what they do.

Set aside discussions of digital cameras, or the new frontier of the multimedia photographer, or anything that is about the mechanical aspect of making pictures rather than the aspect of communicating with a picture.

Sancetta says: "I know I feel better when I've done a good job, made a good picture. If I can go out and make a good picture, something I can be proud of, it makes my whole week."

This book is written under the assumption that you already know how to operate your camera, make the proper exposure, make the simplest of prints or handle digital images on a screen.

A sturdy tripod, the good fortune of a clear night and a good idea of what he wanted were the key ingredients for photographer Alistair Grant's illustration of Comet Hale-Bopp as it streaked over England's Stonehenge in 1997. The travels of the comet as it passed the Bronze Age monuments were recorded on 800 ASA color negative film at 1/30th of a second at f4.

That kind of thrill never really goes away. The most jaded professionals, after particularly tough assignments, still want to see the pictures as soon as possible to see if their ideas worked.

Reporting with a camera. Capturing the instant for others. The "decisive moment." Photojournalism.

It will attempt to take you beyond that. It includes picking the right angle, the right medium, lighting the situation if needed, and a discussion of the philosophies of photographers and how they cover a broad range of assignments.

It will introduce you to the basics of good news photography.

The Look:
Composition, Style, Cropping

Three forces -- composition, style and cropping -- control the look of your photographs.

Composition is the collection of elements in the picture, and how those elements compete for the reader's attention. As the eye tracks across the pictures, the position of those elements, the composition, makes the eye move on or stop and study the image.

By approaching your photography so that the composition -- the look of the picture -- is consistent, you will develop a "style" that identifies those pictures as yours. Cropping is including, or excluding, elements as the picture is made, or later in the photo lab or on the computer screen, or at the editor's desk.

All three disciplines -- composition, style, cropping -- are tough to teach, according to several professional photographers and picture editors. Developing an individual style is a challenge.

Some are successful.

Larry Nighswander was a picture editor at National Geographic magazine before moving to Ohio University to head the university's School for Visual Communication. At the Geographic, he worked with a collection of great photographers who had styles of their own but didn't let these styles stand in the way of communicating.

In fact, they probably elevated the communication.

Opposite page: Taking a step back to emphasize the solitude, using the available light of an ornate New York hotel room, photographer Wyatt Counts made a portrait of sax player Clarence Clemens that lets the reader almost hear the music.

AP photographer Eric Gay combined the right angle with the right lens to draw the reader's eye into his photograph of a lone woman near crosses erected on a hill overlooking Columbine High School in Littleton, Colo. Fifteen people died in a school shooting rampage there in 1999. Gay's photo shows that taking a step back from the scene can sometimes make the picture more powerful than a tight closeup.

"There are a number of photographers," Nighswander says, "like Alex Webb, Bill Allard, Sam Abell and David Harvey, who have sophisticated ways of seeing things that utilize layers within a frame." That layering, according to Nighswander, "gives a photograph depth and, in some cases, hidden compositional elements that make the reader look at the photograph and think about it for just a little while longer."

And, that is good, he says, because "the longer we can captivate someone and make them think about what they are seeing, the better chance we have of them understanding what it is we are trying to say with the photograph."

Newspaper graphics consultant Bob Lynn, who led the emergence of strong photo operations at the Charleston, W.Va., and Norfolk, Va., newspapers, says you might be surprised by just how visually sophisticated your readers are.

"I think the level of sophistication with a lot of readers out there is very high," he says. For instance, "the younger ones have been raised on visuals of all kinds since they were babies. I give readers a heck of a lot more credit than a lot of the editors do."

In fact, according to Lynn, that might be the problem. "My take is that the really conservative people are the editors in the newsroom who don't get out and know what is going on."

At the *The Virginian-Pilot* in Norfolk, Lynn and Alex Burrows, the photo department leaders, got stronger, better pictures into the paper. They were pictures that wouldn't run in some papers and wouldn't have run in the Norfolk paper before their arrival. "Not that they were lewd or anything," Lynn says, "but they were definitely different and definitely not your same old cliches."

AP photographer Robert Bukaty used a slow shutter speed to isolate Nita, the dog, and to give the sensation of speed in this 1999 photo from the back of a pickup truck.

"Some of it is that you have to have the courage to communicate," Lynn says. "You have to shoot it in a new and different way."

But that doesn't mean being arty for art's sake. Lynn remembers some photographers he worked with who were very artistic, but hadn't become journalists yet. Lynn's lesson to them? "If it doesn't communicate anything, it might be great on someone's wall, but it has to tell a story."

Early on in his career, AP photographer Eric Draper picked up some good advice regarding photographic style from a colleague. Draper says the message was simple but to the point. "If an image is pleasing to the eye, it will draw people in, make them stop and look."

And for the second, and just as important, part of that guidance, Draper agrees with the others and says you have to make sure the image doesn't just look good. It has to communicate. "A lot of photographers," Draper says, "are trying to be really creative because they are trying to impress other photographers," and not thinking about the readers.

AP photographer Cliff Schiappa says, "Our prime responsibility is to communicate." And, he adds, "if your style causes static in the signal, in the communication, then you are not a success."

Lynn says the best way for young photographers to learn is to make as many pictures as they can and keep reviewing their work. "A young person should just shoot from the heart and the gut and shoot the pictures that they like."

He feels young photographers have to find their place by making those pictures and not allowing themselves to be molded by others. "If you want to be great," Lynn says, "you need to make your own pictures."

But if you follow that trail, he advises that you should be prepared to move on to pursue the dream. "If you're at a paper that doesn't appreciate it, then you have to move on to a paper that does appreciate it."

AP photo editor Horst Faas, a two-time Pulitzer Prize-winner, got his education in photography in a different way than most. After World War II, Faas and two other men were hired by a photo agency to put back together its picture collection which had been trashed during the war.

Sifting through those thousands of photographs was an incredible experience for Faas. "By looking at a lot of very good pictures," Faas says, "you learned what was good. You would look at them and something would stick in your mind. The telling qualities of the photos we handled was the best journalism instruction I could ever have."

Simply put, Faas "got excited by what you can do with photography."

Washington Post deputy picture editor Michel DuCille says a couple of photographers, Carol Guzy and Eugene Richards, come to mind when he thinks of people who are successful in having a look to their work, but are communicating at a higher level.

AP photographer Jerome Delay made this portrait of a sheik, one of the fabled Blue Men of the desert, while working on a 1997 essay on the group's return to northern Mali after five years in refugee camps in nearby Mauritania.

Guzy's style, DuCille says, is geared more to when she makes the picture. "I know her style is to capture the moment," he says, "but as far as the way she composes the picture, it is different every time."

Richards, according to DuCille, was one of the first photographers to feel comfortable tilting the camera to better compose the elements. DuCille says the result is "dimensional composition, pictures that say more than one thing in one photo, tell more than one story in a single photo."

AP photographer Laura Rauch thinks photographers must make sure their style doesn't become stagnant or simply a habit that can get in the way of communicating.

"You can be a slave to your style," she says. "You have to keep growing, keep getting better." To grow, she says, "your style has to evolve and change and get better. It can't govern you or govern your pictures."

Nighswander says photographers sometimes spend too much time trying to use bits and pieces of other photographers' styles and don't develop a clear style of their own.

"Unfortunately," he says, "we have a tendency to mimic each other. Periodically, we would adopt a photographer as being a visionary and it was not always a well thought out style, but a sloppy style that didn't come out of a well thought out composition."

The result, Nighswander says, is "the message can get obscured and that is problematic."

Instead of losing the reader, Nighswander says photographers and photo editors should be trying to raise the reader's visual sophistication by using more inventive composition, or a more abstract content, "in an effort to make the readers look at the picture and appreciate a sophistication in the composition that might not be evident to the average person."

Newhouse News Service photo chief Toren Beasley likes to take a collection of photos and study them without knowing who shot them. That gets him away from preconceived notions based on a photographer's reputation. "I see how they feel," he says, "see what they do, see how they communicate because what is important is the photograph," not the photographer who made the photo.

Beasley agrees with Nighswander that photographers have a tendency to mimic a popular style and thinks, "there is too much hero worship in photography that leads to copycatting and not to the development of the craft, not the movement of the

J. Scott Applewhite, an AP photographer in Washington, spotted this angle as photographers were moved to a camera platform and then hung back from the pack waiting for the right moment as President Clinton moved toward a podium in 1998.

craft where it can go."

Porter Binks of Sports Illustrated says as photographers starting out, "we've got our hands full just mastering the techniques of the camera and the film and training our eyes to see and our ears to hear. We hardly have time in a lot of our positions to think about style. If something develops over a period of years, that's fine."

Binks thinks the look of a photographer's pictures, created by using certain lenses or certain angles, may be "better defined as a habit that turns into a style."

That style, according to DuCille, should come after a photographer has spent quite a bit of time making pictures and learning the craft. "I'm a little old-fashioned," DuCille says, "in that I think you've got to work many, many, many years before you can even begin to say you've got a style."

DuCille isn't a big fan of people who mindlessly pursue a style.

Style, DuCille says, "is often all about the photographer and not about journalism and not about the subject. So, most of the time when people say they are developing X-kind of style, I'm suspicious because I think it is about them."

That "takes it from being journalism to being art," according to DuCille. "I am a journalist; I just happen to use a camera. I just happen to use my camera to tell a story rather than writing." And, that's not art.

Beasley feels strongly that photographers are artists and that's not a bad thing.

"I am talking about understanding how elements work," Beasely says, "shape, and line and texture, and color, and how things move forward and move back and how they can be used in imparting meaning to a photograph, not just in gaining attention."

"All of those things are from an art background," says Beasley, who came to photography after studying art. "That knowledge is what a photojournalist needs to be good."

Unfortunately, Beasley says, "you don't see a lot of it."

Don't run that artist thing past Hal Buell, the retired former head of the AP's photo service, or you'll have an argument on your hands.

Buell sees it as something that is pretty simple.

"Journalists are not artists," Buell says.

The use of a slow shutter speed to blur the movements of pedestrians and the spiral of a staircase inside a pavilion in Hanover, Germany, draw the reader's eye into this picture by photographer Jens Meyer.

"They shouldn't be artists because artists have a point of view, or at least they should. Journalists are reporters and reporters report what happened."

Buell says Ed White, one of his editors when he was first reporting and writing from Asia, summed it up best: "Tell them what happened." Buell amends that to the words of the photographer. "Tell them what happened, or in our case, show them what happened."

Faas says the key is not to get bogged down in a comparison of photography and art, but to realize "that it is the visual appreciation of things that is important."

Faas has never considered photography to be art. "It is not less," he says. "It is just a different form of expression."

And when it comes to the integrity of the photograph, Faas is in strong agreement with many, including Buell, but says it a different way. "What an artist can do, a photographer should not be permitted to do, and that's to fiddle around with things."

Some say a feeling for composition is either there, or it's not.

"Composition is felt," AP photo editor Bob Daugherty says. "A good picture is felt from the heart. The heart skips a beat at the right moment."

Composition can be a loaded topic, too.

As a helicopter carrying PLO leader Yasser Arafat lands during his first visit to the West Bank after a 1995 pullout by Israeli forces, photographer Jerome Delay of the AP made this picture of crowds protecting themselves from the dust thrown up by the rotors. Although Arafat's arrival was the key, Delay was alert to what was going on around him and took advantage of the moment to make a nice sidebar picture to the visit.

Draper explains that one recent widely adopted compositional technique was to cut off limbs of subjects in pictures.

While some pictures look good with that style of composition, photographers began to overuse the technique. The result? "They are losing the goal of communicating with the average person who is going to see the photo in a newspaper or magazine and

AP photographer Eric Draper used a low angle and a wide angle lens to emphasize the hands in this picture of Texas governor George W. Bush in Englewood, Colo., during his 2000 campaign for president. Draper traveled extensively with Bush during the campaign and used numerous visual devices to break up the routine of the pictures during the year-long marathon of rallies, speeches and sidewalk greetings.

wonder why is that arm floating in the air," Draper says.

Another technique Draper thinks is overused is framing that includes a large out-of-focus object in the foreground. While photographers would talk about the great composition, Draper is afraid readers "just wonder what the blob is."

There are many differing views on cropping, too. Some editors say it is an important tool. Others feel it should be avoided if at all possible.

Burrows, *The Virginian-Pilot* director of photography, is on the side of sparingly

cropping the work of the photographers on his staff. "I think a crop is an opinion," he says, "and that opinion should be expressed like a sentence. You should express it with care."

He thinks the photographer made a decision to crop the scene in the camera when the picture was first made, had another chance to adjust that when the picture was scanned and that the picture editor should take that into account when the photo finally reaches his desk.

Burrows says he tries, "hopefully to get the photo in the paper as close to the photographer's vision as possible. The more you can get the photographer's vision into the paper," he says, "the more it will encourage the photographer to reach out to tell the story."

"It gives the photographer the responsibility," Burrows says. "They are the visual journalist who was at the scene."

At the *Washington Post,* picture selection and cropping are a collaborative effort between the photographers and the photo editors.

"When a photographer comes back from an assignment and we are at the light table," DuCille explains, "I don't grab his film and say I want this one,

The face of Tennessee women's basketball team coach Pat Summitt and the NCAA logo are all that is needed to tell the story of a news conference in this 2000 photo by AP photographer Mark Humphrey.

and this one and this one." Instead, DuCille says, "a conversation begins with what did you see, what were you trying to achieve, what is the story we are trying to tell?"

That leads to a selection of photos and a discussion of crops and both of those discussions make the photographer and picture editor equal partners. But, DuCille says, "if there is a close call on a picture (selection or cropping), the photographers get veto rights over the picture editor." DuCille says it is a rare day when that policy doesn't carry through.

As a side note, DuCille says all of that talking can be beneficial in other ways.

Often, the photographer was the paper's only representative at the scene. The reporter had gathered the facts by phone or from a news release. While talking about the photographer's coverage, things will come out that will enhance or change the reporter's impressions. DuCille says, in that case, the picture editor is the conduit for the newsroom to get that information. And, everyone benefits.

Editors and photographers are talking about the effect of television, advertising and magazines on newspaper photographic styles. They see a blurring of the hard edge that used to define a photograph.

Kenny Irby, the visual journalism group leader at the Poynter Institute in St. Petersburg, Fla., sees continuing evidence of that blurring, particularly in magazines, and wants to make sure journalists don't begin to ease their standards because they think readers aren't concerned.

"What I am most concerned about is that there is a perception that viewers have come to accept the manipulation and don't believe what they see anyway."

Irby, and others, think newspapers, for the most part, try to hold the line on manipulation, but many magazines routinely alter pictures, or in some cases, even create pictures from the parts of several pictures.

"If you are talking about the magazine industry," Irby says, "it is happening everyday. It is challenged everyday. Every magazine you look at, from Vibe magazine to Time magazine, has had covers greatly manipulated."

It can be National Geographic moving pyramids to make a better fit for a cover, or Life magazine taking the pole out the middle of John Paul Filo's famous picture of the young woman screaming over the body of the dead student after the Kent State shootings. It can be Time magazine's alteration of the police mug shot of O.J. Simpson which made him appear more menacing, or even the cover of an issue of Harper's Bazaar which featured a portrait of Princess Caroline of Monaco.

That last one, the Harper's cover, seems innocent enough but looks can be deceiv-

AP electronic photography ethics policy

This is the policy adopted by The Associated Press in 1990:

Electronic imaging raises new questions about what is ethical in the process of editing photographs. The questions may be new but the answers all come from old values.

Simply put, The Associated Press does not alter photographs. Our pictures must always tell the truth.

The electronic picture desk is a highly sophisticated photo editing tool. It takes us out of a chemical darkroom where the subtle printing techniques, such as burning and dodging, have long been accepted as jounalistically sound. Today, these terms are replaced by "image manipulation" and "enchancement." In a time when such broad terms could be misconstrued we need to set limits and restate some basic tenets.

Only the established norms of standard photo printing methods such as burning, dodging, toning and cropping are acceptable. Retouching is limited to removal of normal scratches and dust spots.

The content of a photograph will NEVER be changed or manipulated in any way.

ing, which is the point of all this. The Caroline portrait is actually parts of four different pictures — skin from one photo, hair from another, the face from another and the body from a fourth photo. All combined by a digital magician to make the "perfect" portrait.

Newspapers don't escape without fault.

New York Newsday wanted to feature figure skating rivals Tonya Harding and Nancy Kerrigan on the ice together at the Lillehammer Olympics. Only Harding hadn't arrived in Norway, so it hadn't happened yet. Not a problem. They took separate pictures and combined them for a tabloid front page that, at first glance, had journalists wondering how they had missed the event.

Irby worked at *Newsday's* Long Island home base at the time and says the skating cover, which ran only in the New York City edition of the newspaper, was not the idea of a young journalist or a page designer without journalistic credentials. Instead, he says, it was a veteran high-ranking editor who had the idea, and an illustrator adept with Photo-Shop who was able to take that idea and make it happen.

Or, in a more simple situation, a Topeka *Capital-Journal* photographer, wanting a more perfect basketball picture, electronically moved the ball in his picture of a high school game. But a sharp-eyed reader spot-

> "**W**hat I am most concerned about is that there is a perception that viewers have come to accept the manipulation and don't believe what they see anyway."
>
> — Kenny Irby, the visual journalism group leader at the Poynter Institute in St. Petersburg, Fla.

ted a reflection in the backboard that was out of place and the faked picture was uncovered.

In each case, the magazines and newspapers were trying for a more perfect picture instead of living with what was really there.

In the *Newsday* and Topeka situations, journalists drove the decisions but in many cases that is not true. Some editors think this conceptual edge is more often driven by designers, now showing up in newsrooms in ever-growing numbers, who have no training as journalists and who don't feel bound by the same rules.

"There are a lot of art directors involved now," Buell says, "and they don't have any journalistic sense. They don't understand any of these things that we are talking about." Even worse, he says, "they'll tell you they do but I don't think they do or they wouldn't do some of the things they do."

Irby agrees. "The mass influence of Madison Avenue design thinking, and not journalistic integrity and accuracy has had a major impact," he says. "You see lots of designers in newsrooms who are very gifted at design and typography creating a mood and imagination on a page who do things that are not in line with the traditional values of journalism."

Burrows believes the best defense is a vigilant newsroom. "We want to be honest in a news photograph, just as in a story." From his experience, Burrows thinks, "while designers may try to push the limits, there are enough good journalists to keep an eye on it and call them on it" when they push those limits too much.

Some editors think simply being able to do documentary photography is no longer the only tool or technique of photographic style. Illustrative and conceptual photography is another style that is becoming increasingly important.

But, Burrows isn't so fast to embrace a style that would lead us away from journalism, to a blurring of the edges of what is real and what isn't.

> Conceptual has been defined as whimsy and fantasy, and documentary as reportage and observation.

"The photo illustration should be real obvious that it is one. With news photography, it should be straight and honest and to the point," he says. "It can be artfully shot but not tampered with or manipulated." There shouldn't be any way to confuse the two.

Buell saw a good example during a recent Christmas season.

A newspaper had a picture of a gift-wrapped box with two tiny people overshadowed by it. The picture ran with a story about being overwhelmed by gift giving during the holidays.

"Clearly this is a manipulated picture and anybody who looks at it knows that is a manipulated picture and knows that it is a trick." But, he adds, "the problem comes as that obvious trick, that obvious manipula-tion, that almost caricature or cartoon begins to move toward being more and more real."

Buell feels strongly about this. He says editors need to be alert the "further you move down that spectrum," from the Christmas shopping illustration to something that isn't so obvious. "Is it real, or not real," the reader might wonder, says Buell.

And, don't try to convince him that a simple label will help.

"Newspapers make a big mistake," he says. "They think if they put a 6-point agate line under the picture that says it is a photo illustration that they are off the hook. That's a classic journalistic cop-out. Nobody reads that stuff and they probably don't understand it if they do read it."

Another example cited by Buell is a portrait of Nicole Brown Simpson, the slain former wife of football star O.J. Simpson. While the case was in the headlines, a supermarket tabloid altered a portrait of her to make her face look bruised and swollen, with a black eye.

"It was a manipulation," Buell says, but unlike the Christmas example it wasn't so apparent.

"Down in the caption they made short reference to it being artificial. Here is this thing on the supermarket counter and two-thirds the size of the front page is this photo and down in the caption is some explanation of how that came about. That's a cop-out, plain and simple."

AP photographer Eric Gay used a wide angle lens to show the patterns of the cracked earth, and a dog helps to break up that pattern, in a picture illustrating the effect of a drought in spring 2000 near China Spring, Texas. Gay shot what was there, not setting up a picture, and waited for the right moment.

Conceptual has been defined as whimsy and fantasy, and *documentary* as reportage and observation.

Burrows thinks this new style of illustration photography will only slowly begin to creep into news pages, destined more for the feature sections. "I think newspapers are pretty conservative in their approach in the news pages and that is justified."

But he sees that being tested. "A photographer is always reaching to make better, more visual pictures," Burrows says, "stretching the envelope, while editors are trying to slow that move."

Burrows is concerned about this possible confusion, not wanting to "disturb the reader with gimmicks in the news pages. You have more liberty in the features department, changes come more easily there than in the news pages. Feature sections are more wide open," he says, "and readers now sense the difference."

Beasley isn't so sure that whimsy and fantasy are the best description for conceptual. And, acknowledging that this view might not be popular, he's not even sure there ever really was documentary photography.

"I really think that documentary photography never existed," he says. "I think that everything you have seen that we have labeled as documentary is either photographs without meaning or, if you really look at it, since there was a person there who decided to organize these particular elements in a particular way, it is not documentary."

He explains, "What I'm talking about is not taking things and inventing something, like photo illustration. We are not creating things that don't exist. We are talking about the interpretation of things that do exist."

Beasley says he isn't advocating setting up pictures, just acknowledging that by including or not including something in the frame, or using some other technique to highlight or minimize some aspect of the picture, it is not a straight piece of documentation.

"Go ahead and organize the elements," he says. "You can do the things that give people the sense of what you are seeing. It is not that what you are seeing isn't related to the reality, it is."

This emphasis on composition and content, coupled with the new ideas and techniques that photojournalists are being exposed to, is leading to more photographs becoming visual statements, with the imprint and input of the photographer in each picture.

That is to be expected, Beasley feels, and it is truthful to what happened. "You want people to live in the picture," he says. "If someone is jumping for joy, you want the reader to feel that joy. You want the reader to feel what you feel." According to Beasley, the photographer is saying, "I'm here and I am your eyes to this, and this is

what I see. This is how I feel about it."

Again, it isn't that the photograph isn't telling the truth, it is just telling the truth of what the photographer wanted to relate.

The sense of "style" isn't new to news photography.

AP photographer Rusty Kennedy says W. Eugene Smith's style is timeless and has been an example to many photojournalists. "I think in the beginning, most people that I knew who were serious about photojournalism wanted to emulate people like W. Eugene Smith and the photo-essay concept. You got a seed of an idea and tried to develop it, and you tried to have a set of pictures with at least one really strong one."

"Many of the things he did, like the rural doctor, you could have used those ideas on anyone," Kennedy says. "Real dramatic black and white photography."

"I think that you have to be careful when you are talking about having a style," Indianapolis freelancer Mary Ann Carter says, "because the job of a photojournalist is to tell a story and communicate. If you forgo that goal for the sake of a style, you're not doing what is important."

Carter explains that "it's OK to have a style, like using a blue gel or using an extremely wide-angle lens, but if your style precludes you from being a communicator, maybe it is not such a good style for a photojournalist. Sometimes you have to adapt your style to the story you are covering," she says. "Photojournalists have to be able to shoot a lot of different things -- sports, news, and features."

She warns there is a danger to adapting a style that has no flexibility. "One day you may be shooting something where a blue gel or a wide-angle lens is fine, but the next day it might not work at all."

Des Moines Register director of photography John Gaps III feels he adapts his style to the circumstances of the coverage he's

do that for myself," Gaps says, using "a tighter lens, a wider lens, a different angle." But on a breaking news assignment, "when there is a lot flying and I'm right on deadline," he says, "I try to get what an editor would want to see. Then, when I've got

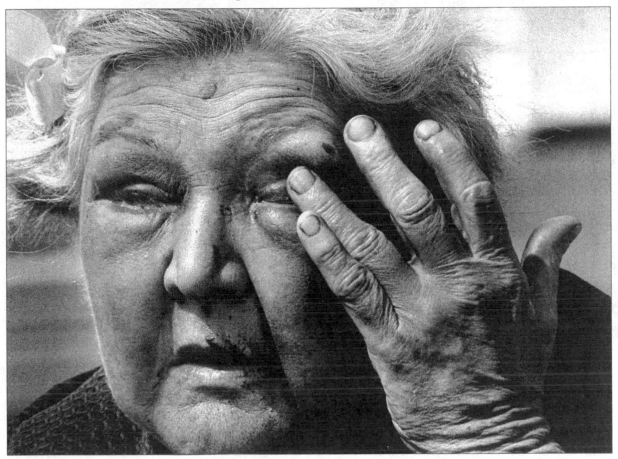

The style of legendary photojournalist W. Eugene Smith inspires AP photographer Rusty Kennedy who used Smith's black and white essay technique on this portrait of a homeless woman in Philadelphia. It was part of a larger group of pictures he did in 1974 on that community before homelessness was a national topic. Using available light and working at slow shutter speeds, Kennedy's picture captures every detail and tells the story of the woman's tough existence.

involved in at the moment. "By now," he says, "I have two different ways of shooting: when you take pictures for yourself, and when you take pictures for someone else."

On a sports assignment, "I always try to

that clear, I say, 'How do I see things?'"

Gaps' early photography also was influenced by the work of W. Eugene Smith, and several photographers from the region where he attended college. "W. Eugene Smith was everything, but also Rich Clarkson, Jim Richardson and Brian Lanker in Topeka. I got exposed to that group's photography a lot because my college professor would invite them up for lectures."

Daugherty boils his style down to one

Using a low angle and strong backlighting, AP photographer John Gaps III captured the fragility of a young boy with his father in Somalia in 1992. The two were traveling to a clinic for medical treatment for the child.

thing — simplicity. "I don't like to introduce too many elements into a picture."

At the risk of being called single-minded in that respect, Daugherty says his photography mirrors the approach he tries to take in life. "I don't like to have too many loose ends, in my work, and in my life. A good picture is generally a single subject, not a lot of loose elements."

Carter says she defines her style as a personal approach to the people she photographs. "My style is to respect people and

try not to put them in situations that denigrate them or belittle them." She says she takes a simple approach. "I think you have to treat people the way you want to be treated." She calls this "a gentle determination."

Carter also is exposing herself to other ways of forging the visual makeup of her pictures. "The way I'm trying to improve my eye overall is that I took a drawing class, and I study the techniques of artists," she says, "and I look at photographers who are not photojournalists. And I try to look at photographers who are better than I am and see what they are doing and try to spark my mind in those directions."

She says that the drawing class has taught her the theory of getting into a right-brain mode. Carter explains that your brain operates in two sections, with the right brain handling artistic functions and the left brain handling logical functions. "Photography is a right-brain activity. It's creative," she says, "and the class was based on getting into the right-brain mode. If I can do that, it should help my photography."

AP photographer Susan Ragan credits her art studies with giving her a sense of composition. "From my art background, I think about composition and beauty and balance that may not be so evident to other photographers." Ragan's training includes a Fine Arts master's degree in drawing and painting. She didn't take up photography until she had several years of art training behind her.

"Maybe that made me sensitive to different pictures," she says. "I think I have a sense of composition and light from that training." Ragan says, for instance, "I know when there is Rembrandt light on someone from the art training I've had."

The use of smash closeups, isolation with long lenses, strong lighting techniques and different perspectives give pictures a different look. Some of these techniques are rooted in painting, others in the styles of avant-garde photographers.

Old style, or new, good composition means pictures that are interesting to look at. That's the simple definition.

J. Bruce Baumann, of the Evansville, Ind., *Courier and Press,* sums it up with a no-frills explanation. "If something doesn't

Like Gaps on the opposite page, Eric Draper of the AP used the techniques of a low angle and a dramatic sky but in a lighter situation—a youngster playing basketball in a rural New Mexico town in 1998. The picture was part of an essay by Draper on the wide open spaces of the Southwest.

need to be in a picture, it shouldn't be there. You accomplish that by where you stand and what lens you use."

Nighswander says that beginning photojournalists should start with the basics of composition. "There is no doubt in my mind that one of the first things a young photographer needs is a command of these visual devices."

Those "visual devices" are the concepts

Visual checklist

Ohio University School of Visual Communication director Larry Nighswander has compiled this checklist for the photojournalist.

Does the photograph have technical excellence?

❏ Sharp focus ❏ Good contrast ❏ Correct color balance

Does the photograph have compositional creativity?

❏ Dominant foreground, contributing background ❏ Reflection

❏ Introducing disorder into an ordered situation ❏ Panning

❏ Introducing color into a monochromatic scene ❏ Juxtaposition

❏ Rule of thirds composition ❏ Decisive moment

❏ Framing ❏ Linear perspective

❏ Selective focus ❏ Silhouette

Does the photograph have any editorial relevance or merit?

1) Is the photo active or passive?

2) Is the photograph of something no one has ever seen before or is it a unique or interesting photo of something everyone has seen?

3) Is the photo style and the writing style consistent?

4) Does the photo communicate quicker, stronger, better or more eloquently than a simple sentence could describe?

5) Does the photo have visual content, or stop short at story elevation?

6) Does the photo go beyond the trite and the obvious?

7) Does the photo contain essential information to help the reader understand the story?

8) Does the photo have enough impact to move the reader?

9) Is the photo clean, interesting, and well-composed enough to stand on its own?

10) Does the caption information answer who, what, when, where and why, along with other required information (e.g. age and hometown)?

11) Are both the photo and the caption information objective and accurate accounts of what happened?

12) Is the photo mindless documentation?

13) Does the photo communicate effectively? Photos should either move, excite, entertain, inform or help the reader understand a story.

Among the visual devices a photographer can use is perspective. AP photographer Mark Terrill mounted a camera over the arena floor to capture Shaquille O'Neal peeking through the net while going for a rebound in the 2000 NBA Finals.

that make a picture more interesting to look at. Ideas like the rule of thirds, linear perspective, framing, the "decisive moment," selective focus, controlled depth of field, perspective, and others should be in the photographer's basic "tool kit."

Nighswander has identified fifteen devices that have an effect on the look of a photojournalist's pictures.

If you take an extremely creative photo, Nighswander says, and dissect it, "it can contain four or five creative devices. Each helps strengthen the power of the photograph."

He says no matter how much experience you have, these visual devices can make your pictures better. "Every time I take a picture, these things click through my mind. I'm always thinking, which ones can I use?"

Carter says an easy way to improve a photograph's composition is to merely change perspectives. That's one of the visual devices.

"You have to move around a lot," she says. "You have to watch shooting everything from eye level." You can shoot "on a ladder, or on your knee, or on your belly" to get a different view.

For instance, Carter says some of the pictures her children shot when they were growing up are interesting, just because they are shot from a different perspective. "When you give a kid a camera, they are going to shoot everything at their eye level. That's your knee level, and it's an interesting view."

Carter says photographers should vary their perspectives as much as possible. "Too many pictures from the same perspective makes the reader lose interest," she says. In fact, she says, using any of the visual devices too often will dull the reader's response.

Burrows believes that knowing how the picture is going to be used will help the photographer get the most mileage out of those creative tools.

These three AP photographers use different compositional techniques to draw the reader's eye. John Moore's 1996 photo of workers preparing rice in the kitchen of an Afghan orphanage (top) uses the strong shaft of light to bring the reader to the workers and their kettle. Eric Draper uses silhouette and framing techniques in a photo of a 1998 manhunt in the Utah back country (above right) and Laura Rauch employs a long lens to isolate the action at a 1999 rodeo (left).

The first thing that is important for the photographer heading out on an assignment, Burrows says, is "to know what you are shooting for — A1, inside, secondary play, the feature section. You have to know the audience you're aiming for."

He says you should make different kinds of pictures for different uses. "For instance, if you are shooting an assignment for a column," Burrows says, "you might be shooting for a small picture. So you would want to go for an impact image." On the other hand, "if you are shooting for the main picture on A1, and they'll use a four-column picture, you can shoot a looser photograph."

However, if the newspaper doesn't generally display pictures that size and that same assignment is going to be used slightly smaller, it could change the composition of the picture needed. "If it is a three-column instead, you have to shoot for a little more impact," he explains. "The bigger the general size, the more flexibility on the looseness. A small picture needs more impact."

To give that smaller picture greater impact, Burrows recommends that the photographer concentrate on the person's face and have fewer, simpler elements. He says

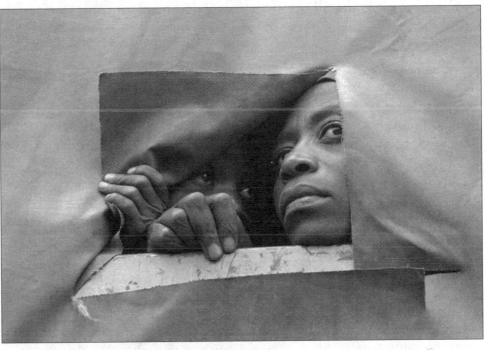

Framing the scene with a wide angle lens and working close to his subject, AP photographer David Guttenfelder made this picture of Rwandan refugees peering through the hole in a rain cover on a United Nations truck in 1996. Guttenfelder often used the wide angle lens and worked close to his subjects when he was in Africa, but had to change his style to reflect the different attitudes of people in Asia.

that is important on a small picture so the reader's eye won't be confused with the clutter.

On the picture to be played larger, a looser composition works. "You still have to keep an uncluttered picture," Burrows says. But he says that the elements of the picture don't have to have the same boldness, the same impact, that is needed when the picture is going to be player smaller.

The best of both worlds, Burrows says, "is to have the real impact in a large picture. "That's the maximum impact."

AP photographer Harry Cabluck thinks there is an easy way for photographers to improve the impact of pictures. It's the choice of the lens they'll use.

Cabluck says you can shoot the same scene in a more readable manner by using a longer lens, even if you have to take a position farther from your subject. The subject will be crisper, because the depth of field is not so great, and the scene will be more pleasing to the eye.

AP photographer Jerome Delay prefers to use fixed focal length lenses. "I don't like zooms because they make people lazy. You don't move, all of your pictures look the same."

"Your perspective is different if you take two steps forward or two steps backward. Standing still makes for stagnant pictures," Delay says.

Unlike Cabluck, Delay likes the look he gets from a wide angle lens. Delay's lens of choice, when the situation doesn't demand the use of a long lens, is the 24 mm lens on a digital camera. He believes that gives him

the same look as a 35 mm lens on a film camera, "that is closer to the way the eye sees a scene."

He doesn't think this preferred use of one lens compromises his ability to get the

AP photographer Jerome Delay combines a digital camera, a 24 mm lens and a style of getting close to his subjects and filling his frame to produce eye-catching photographs like this one of ethnic Albanian refugees as they leave their home in Kosovo in 1999. Delay doesn't think his preference for the wide angle lens compromises his photography.

best image. "If it doesn't fit in the 24, I step back. If there is a wall, then maybe I don't make the picture. If the eye can't see the picture, the camera can't either!"

Another lesson from Cabluck's days at the Fort Worth *Star-Telegram* is "to shoot vertically as often as possible and have a camera that is easy to hold vertically because the newspaper pages are vertical and it is easier to do the makeup with a vertical in mind."

Cabluck says photographers sometimes

forget who they are shooting for. "The reader," Cabluck says, "that's who we are doing it for."

Others say that too much of anything — horizontals, verticals, closeups, wide shots

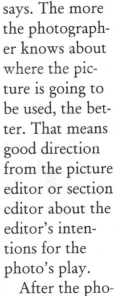

Often, while chasing a story that goes on for several days, photographers find it hard to stay alert and look for unique pictures. Not so for AP photographer Eric Draper who followed Mark McGwire on his chase to break the home run record in 1998. Because he paid attention when McGwire wasn't at bat, he got this offbeat picture of him cooling off in the dugout before taking the field.

photographer needs to compose the story with different perspectives and focal lengths to give visual variety to the story."

It all goes back to the guidance the photographer had before shooting the assignment, Burrows says. The more the photographer knows about where the picture is going to be used, the better. That means good direction from the picture editor or section editor about the editor's intentions for the photo's play.

After the photographer has decided on an approach to photography, and used the visual devices to compose a picture, the deci-

— should be avoided.

When assigned to more than one picture on a given subject, Nighswander stresses, the still photographer "ought to think like a film director, making closeup, medium and overall views." This variety will result in a visually appealing picture story.

"Just as a film director wouldn't shoot from one perspective and with one focal length lens," Nighswander says, "a still

sion has to be made whether to use the picture as a "full-frame" image, exactly as it was made in the camera, or if the framing needs to be altered.

This decision sometimes falls on the photographer, other times on an editor.

When it is decided that a picture should be cropped, some want the photographer to have and exercise that option. Others believe it is the editor's responsibility to make that decision.

Nighswander says the photographer should think about how the picture should look right from the start. "There are basically three times you can crop the picture: when you shoot it, when you print or scan it, and when you send it to the back shop."

While they are shooting, photographers should be trying to make a picture that is as flexible as possible. "You can always crop tighter in the darkroom or on the picture desk, but you can't crop looser," Nighswander says. "You can't add information," once the picture is made.

"You really need to think, not only like photographers, but like designers," he says. Photographers should be aware of problems they can help solve by shooting with a variety of compositions. Nighswander says there's "nothing worse than having everything shot from the same perspective and in the same format (horizontal or vertical)." That takes away an editor's flexibility.

And he has a message to those photographers who are reluctant to think of themselves as picture editors. "Every time you shoot, you are exercising your opinion as an editor."

Carter isn't one of the reluctant ones. "Most pictures can be improved by cropping," she says. "Sometimes I will crop in the camera, and it is the most pleasing, but nine times out of ten it can be improved by cropping in the darkroom. I think intelligent cropping will improve the readership of the image."

Burrows thinks that too much cropping on the picture desk can take away from the photographer's message. "I'm in favor of less heavy-handed editing," he says. "You don't have to put your finger on every picture." Burrows suggests that an editor talk to the photographer before cropping a picture.

"The photographer had a special meaning when he took that photograph," Burrows says, "and you have to know the photographer and how he presents his pictures." He compares it to editing a story. "You have to communicate with the photographer about the crop. Learn to ask what the photographer wants to say with the picture," Burrows says, "and if the photographer has a definite opinion about the picture, it is up to the photo editor to judge if the editing will add or take away from the photograph's message."

AP photographer Eric Gay used a long lens but framed the picture to include some needed atmosphere while covering this 2000 memorial service, which marked the fifth anniversary of the deadly explosion at the federal building in Oklahoma City.

Burrows says every photographer has different feelings about the editing process. "Some don't care, others like to talk about the cropping," he says.

Nighswander takes a simple, straightforward approach. "I think you should crop out anything that doesn't add content or information or mood. That's important," he says. "I know a lot of editors can't understand the importance of leaving any kind of open feeling. That's often what gives mood to the picture. Sometimes a little space around the picture can give you a feeling, even if it may be subtle."

Conceptual images, illustrations, feet cut off, dominant foregrounds, subjectivity as a personal style. The old rules don't always apply anymore when you're talking about style, composition and cropping.

Nighswander is not so sure that getting rid of the rules is so bad. He's for having guidelines, not rules, for dealing with content and display, because he says every day is a little different at a newspaper.

"I try to keep an open mind on all that because there are so many variables," he

AP's Eric Risberg found a painter doing some last-minute work on a new entertainment complex wall before its formal opening. By not cropping too tightly, Risberg's photo gives you a feel for the facility while also drawing your eye into the picture with the weight of the silhouetted painter.

says. "If I was too structured in my thinking, I might limit myself when I go to put my page together."

Nighswander issues a challenge to newspapers that are too structured when he says, "I want to give my reader a variety of images. I don't want the reader to be able to anticipate what I will give them."

"You can't get yourself to where you are saying no to too many things."

News:
Sensitivity, Thinking, Instinct and Curiosity

Covering news assignments calls for a case of curiosity. Sensitivity. Some thinking. And instinct. Make that a lot of curiosity, sensitivity, thought, persistence and instinct.

David Longstreath says a college professor opened his eyes to one of the main ingredients you need to cover the news. Longstreath says the professor asked his class, "What makes a good reporter?" The discussion went on for some time. Talk of equipment and training dominated the discussion. But, Longstreath says, "the bottom line was curiosity. That has always struck me." Longstreath says you can't go wrong if, as you approach a news scene, "you ask yourself what is it about this that is interesting."

Veteran photographers agree there is no way to be taught news coverage techniques. You really have to learn them by going out and doing it.

"Shooting hard news is like going fishing or hunting. You have to have patience," Longstreath says, "but you also have to have street smarts." There are no short cuts to learning the news business. "There are no tricks. You have to work at it. Like playing the piano, you keep practicing and practicing and practicing."

AP photographer Mark Duncan says your aim should be to "look beyond the

Opposite page: A long night on stakeout duty came to a head quickly for AP photographer Wilfredo Lee as government agents stormed a Miami house in 2000, then came running out with six-year-old Elian Gonzalez. Lee only had a moment to react, but his photograph shows the intensity of the moment.

obvious. Look for something more compelling with more emotion." Photographer Eric Risberg of the AP agrees. He says sports and news are alike in that "better pictures aren't always the main moments, but the moments after."

Ed Reinke, an AP photographer, agrees with that approach. "In news, as in sports, reaction often brings the very best pictures. When the action is important, often the reaction is even more important."

Risberg compares news to sports this way: "We all look for the great play," he says, "but the best picture is sometimes after the great play happens, the reaction. By learning that in sports, you can carry that over to news. At news events, we often get the peak moments, but we should use the sports approach and look for the moment after the peak."

Sports Illustrated photographer John Biever, whose early photography work was at the *Milwaukee Journal* where he covered a wide variety of assignments, says he sees a lot of similarities between covering a sports event and covering a political campaign. "There are just similar moments in both," Biever says. "Either way, you are looking for emotion and the peak moment."

The AP's Elise Amendola says covering news is akin to playing in a spirited game of basketball. At the news event, like the basketball game, "a lot is happening. Sights, movements and sounds are swirling around you. It's imperative to focus on your images as you shoot," she says. "Try to relegate the sounds, movement and your emotional response to the background."

As an aside, Amendola plays basketball regularly. "I like to play basketball," she says, "not only to keep in shape physically but to work my mind and my vision. Threading a pass through a swarming defense that leads a teammate to the hoop is good practice for my timing and for seeing peripherally."

Risberg says the good photojournalist doesn't wrap up the coverage after the obvious pictures are made. The thinking photographer, he says, "will go back a few hours later, a day later, or a week later, when there are often different and good pictures to be made."

Part of that is looking for solid topics.

J. Bruce Baumann of the Evansville, Ind., *Courier and Press,* thinks that contests, and the books that are produced showing contest winners, are making it too easy for photographers to follow someone else's lead instead of finding their own issues and subjects to photograph.

For instance, Baumann says, if a big winner is pictures of poverty, several photo essays on the topic show up soon after. "Why aren't the 'photojournalists' in this country doing the research and going out and seeing what is the problem?"

AP photographer Cliff Schiappa sees good and bad in contests.

"I think that there is good and evil in contests," he says. "Good in that it forces you to reflect on the past year and see if you have grown. The bad is that people copy what is successful and don't grow themselves."

J. Scott Applewhite of the AP's Washington photo staff enjoys a different kind of photo contest. Each morning, he checks

Billowing clouds of anti-personnel gas and police intent on clearing the streets of demonstrators were just part of what AP photographer Beth Keiser faced as she tried to cover the World Trade Organization talks in Seattle in 1999.

Sancetta of the AP says keeping on your toes pays off. "It's so important when you're at an event to be alert, to keep yourself so tapped in."

Part of that alertness is not talking yourself out of trying something. You have to guard against that. "Experience is worth a lot in a photojournalism situation," says Laura Rauch of the AP. "But, if you are trying to be more creative sometimes, experience might hinder you because you might not try something."

In the back of your mind, she says, you are thinking, "Oh, I've done that before and it didn't work." Fight that feeling, she says. "It might work today because you are better at it. If you've got the time, sometimes it is better to push yourself past what experience already tells you."

Longstreath, based in Bangkok, often faces assignments throughout Southeast Asia where tensions are high and stories are often based on a historical perspective.

One of those situations is the backdrop for Longstreath's photo of Cambodian despot Pol Pot after his death.

"You have to have some perspective on history to understand how important this was," Longstreath says. "This was the last despot of the 20th century. I wasn't taking no for an answer, and I wasn't coming back until I had it."

the newsstand to see how his pictures from an event the previous day stack up against the work of other photographers who were there.

"It is nice to know if you did a good enough job to have your pictures on page one above the fold," Applewhite says.

When you are on an assignment, Amy

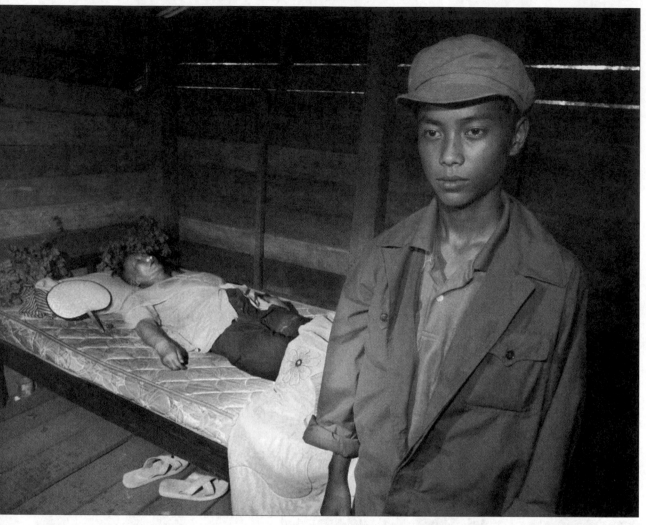

AP photographer David Longstreath knew it was "time to go to work," when he was escorted into a jungle hut to view the remains of former Cambodian ruler Pol Pot in 1998. "We walked inside and there he was," says the Bangkok-based photographer. He only had a few minutes to capture the scene before hustling back to the border to avoid fighting in the area.

Longstreath and his AP colleagues had been seeking an interview with the reclusive dictator for more than a year. And Longstreath was planning a trip to the area along the Thailand-Cambodia border, where it was believed Pol Pot was in hiding, when word came that he might be dead.

During a speedy five-hour drive that followed, Longstreath and an AP reporter worked the cell phone almost continuously with sources and government officials, first trying for confirmation, then trying to arrange transit across the border.

"Every fifteen minutes, we would call them again," Longstreath says. Over the course of the long drive, "we wore them down to the point where they finally said 'Can you be there by a certain time?' When we got to the checkpoint where we needed to be, a sergeant there hadn't gotten the word."

After some discussions, which grew heated at times, the sergeant checked with higher-ups and soon the AP team was on its way.

At the border, Longstreath was put in a car with some local journalists for a short drive across on a dirt road through the jungle. "We drove about 300 yards and the Khmer Rouge [Pol Pot's army] picked us up," Longstreath remembers. "They were waiting for us."

As they led Longstreath and a television crew down a path, "They were very nervous. They kept telling us, 'Don't get off the path,' because it was heavily mined."

Longstreath and the others came into a clearing and were led to a hut. "I walked inside," he says, "and there he was. He was laying on a cot. He had his famous fan with him. He was dead. It was like, 'OK, time to go to work.' This took all of three minutes inside the hut."

There was automatic-weapons fire and shelling in the area and Longstreath knew he had to make his pictures and get back to the border.

"We were very nervous because there was clearly a battle going on down the road somewhere," he says. Longstreath and the other journalists made a quick sprint for the border. Once he was back across the border, Longstreath had his driver take him a short distance to a gas station where he set up his satellite phone and laptop and filed his pictures.

According to Applewhite, paying attention and spotting something you want, then being persistent enough to get it, is the key. "I'm not a gifted photographer," he says, "but I am persistent. I never go back empty-handed. That has helped me more than any other quality."

Longstreath says sometimes it's tough to pay attention. "When other people are talking or joking," he says, "it's better to bear down and think. And look at things, rethink your approach and look again."

Eric Draper of the AP agrees. "I see a lot of photographers missing things because they are being social," he says, "and their heads aren't in the story." Draper says there's no reason not to say hello. "I'll meet and greet other photographers," he explains, "but most of the time I keep my concentration, keep working, keep my eyes peeled for a picture."

And use every tool and technique in your mind -- or your camera bag -- to help you make better news pictures.

For instance, you normally want to use as fast a shutter speed as possible on news assignments in order to "freeze" the action. But to show the fury of a fire fed by 80-

Photographers learn new lessons daily

Amy Sancetta: "Be kind to the people that you work with, your colleagues or the subjects of your photos. The subjects may be opening a part of their life to you that they've not shared with others."

To show the fury of a fire fed by 80-mile-per-hour winds, AP photographer Doug Pizac used a tripod to steady the camera and a slow shutter speed to emphasize the wind-whipped flames. Photographers not only have to know what tools they have at their disposal, but also how to use them to help tell the story they are trying to communicate.

mile-an-hour winds, Doug Pizac used a long exposure to better tell the story. Pizac put his camera on a tripod, and made a half-second exposure to capture the intensity. Then he popped in a strobe to light the fireman.

A case of using the tools available -- a slow shutter speed, a tripod and a strobe -- to make an eye-catching, informative picture.

You have to use those tools wisely while facing a tight deadline, a seemingly impossible coverage situation, or circumstances that have you or your skills stretched to the limit. And avoid letting those tools overwhelm you.

Applewhite says he always tries to keep it in perspective. "It's the image, that's what counts. You can get bogged down with computers and lenses and cell phones. But, if you don't have the picture, nothing else matters."

The bottom line for Applewhite? "When people put their quarters in the newsrack and look at your picture, they don't care what it took to get it. It either sings, or it doesn't."

Reinke cautions that there are boundaries to watch in news that don't exist in feature photography. "As for photojournalism, and

I emphasize the word journalism, we make photographs from the circumstances we are given and we don't try to alter those circumstances."

The simplest situation can be a test of trust.

Wilmington, Del., *News-Journal* director of photography Jeanne Mell says her photo staff strictly follows a rule not to set up photos. But, every day, they have assignments where the subject asks them, "What do you want me to do?" The answer is for the person to do what he or she would be doing if the photographer wasn't standing there.

you would want it, but you live with it," Mell says, because you know at least it is an honest picture.

Washington Post picture editor Michel DuCille says his staff faces the same kind of situation.

AP photographer Robert Bukaty wanted to go beyond news conferences and orchestrated photo opportunities when a giant ice storm knocked down lines and power to a wide area of Maine in 1998. Driving through the darkened area he found a house with a lantern shining in a window. For the four days since the storm struck, the elderly couple there had been using a battery-powered radio, the lantern, a kerosene heater and a camp stove to get along without electricity.

But it isn't as simple as that. The subject already had it in his or her mind that the photographer is willing to set up a picture. And, that gets to the heart of the credibility of the paper. Because if people are around when a picture is set up, they may think that almost any picture has been set up.

"The public," she says, "just doesn't understand the concept of reality journalism."

"Sometimes the picture isn't as clean as

"I think that we need to recognize it," DuCille says, "and do all we can to get people to understand what we do." DuCille tells subjects he doesn't want them to "fake anything" for the paper's photographers. "If anything," he tells them, "I want you to go about your duties so I can capture the essence of what you are doing."

DuCille thinks we can win that uphill battle to keep readers' trust. "The best thing you can do," he says, "is to be totally honest with your subjects, with your readers, and be totally honest as a person practicing journalism."

It's easy to get frustrated when circumstances don't work out as well as you had hoped, but AP photo editor Bob Daugherty suggests moving along to the next item on the agenda.

A misty night and the harsh lighting at the perimeter fence at a Tennessee prison are the tableau for a photo of anti-death penalty protesters silently lighting candles while waiting for a 1999 execution. AP photographer Ed Reinke relied on available light to help tell the story of isolation.

"I guess you have got to avoid getting down on yourself," he says. "I have a thing I run through my mind when things are going badly: Try not to worry about that over which I have no control." He says worrying about a change in plan or a mistake in shooting can hurt you later. "If you're fretting about something, you're not going to be in the right frame of mind when the moment happens. You've got to avoid getting down after mistakes." After you've had a mental or mechanical lapse, Daugherty says, you just have "to come back and do what you do the best."

Daugherty tells a story to illustrate his point about being calm and making the best pictures you can. During a long-ago presidential campaign, Daugherty nervously looked around a rally and jumped every time there was an outburst of applause or a reaction in the crowd.

Veteran UPI photographer Frank Cancellare, also on the assignment, looked over and said, "Kid, you can't shoot the sound." Daugherty calls it some of the best advice he ever got. Do what you do best. Make pictures when there is something to make pictures of.

Hard news often isn't pleasant. Many times you're working in an explosive atmosphere. Someone may have been injured or killed in an accident, people may have lost their life's work in a fire, or opposing groups may be emotionally charged.

It's a heavy pressure, the pressure to make the best possible picture, balanced with sensitivity toward the people in your pictures, measured against the thin line of involvement by the photographer.

Des Moines Register director of photography John Gaps III says it is important for editors to trust their staff, and let them know of that trust, so the photographers don't feel pressure to make something that might not really be there.

"If you start not accepting that they didn't come back with something," Gaps says, "you put pressure on them to do something that perhaps isn't as truthful."

For the photographer's part of that understanding, Gaps says they have to pledge to be truthful in their reporting. "You have to be faithful to what is truthful," he says. "Always returning to what is truthful, what has happened in the scene, will sooner or later result in a factual still photograph."

Gaps warns that you don't want to let tactics -- lighting, lensing, etc. -- get in the way. "I am going to let the scene truthfully happen. I am going to truthfully portray it and then I will play to my strengths," is what each photographer should be saying, according to Gaps.

And if all of that doesn't work, the editor should accept that the photographer failed but failed while trying.

Risberg says he depends on his instincts as he quickly sizes up a news scene and tries to find a middle ground. "News is the most instinctive thing for me. It is really challenging. You can't really prepare for it. You've got to rely on instinct."

Risberg also advises, "When I'm doing news, I travel light and don't shoot too much film. I try to think, and not get caught up in the event. I distance myself."

Draper also subscribes to the travel-light approach. "Usually when I'm out," he says, "I don't carry a camera bag. Instead, I carry

Although AP photographer J. Scott Applewhite was in position to cover the landing of the presidential helicopter in New York in 1999, he was ready to react with a wide angle lens when he saw a member of the local police security line brace himself against the rotor wash.

two camera bodies ready to go, ready to fire at all times, with enough disk space so I'm not caught short."

He's ready, he says, "just in case I see something to grab a shot of." That way, nothing will get away from him. "I don't want to be surprised," he says. "Moments happen so quickly and once they are gone, there is no way to get them back."

"Having your camera ready gets you in the ballpark," he says, "but you also have

AP photographer Stephan Savoia moved away from the pack for an alternate angle and a good picture of presidential candidate Sen. John McCain during a 2000 campaign stop at a town meeting in Newberry, S.C.

to be mentally ready."

Many photographers subscribe to the theory that there's a spot called X in any news situation. If you can figure out where that spot is and manage to be there, you've got the key picture.

"I tend to cover a lot of territory with my eyes," Draper says, "and I ask a lot of questions, too, to get to the bottom of the story." Draper wants to know what the story is, what is important. If he can quickly figure that out, he's got a good start on finding the 'X.'

Sometimes a photographer has a pretty good idea where that spot is but authorities might have a different idea.

Draper was on assignment in Macedonia photographing refugees from the war in Kosovo as they were being bused to an airport boarding area. As he was being ushered away by airport police, because they thought photographers had made enough pictures, Draper says, "I saw this face in the very last window. It stopped me in my tracks."

The police were shouting for Draper and others to leave. But Draper hung back, even though they were shouting and pulling on him, and made his picture. "All of this stuff was going on behind me while I was making the picture," he says. "I had to hold on as long as possible to get the moment."

Draper only had an instant in which it all came together. "It happened pretty quickly and I knew I had something powerful."

While covering a demonstration in Kansas City, Schiappa would make a few frames then get chased away by police. "The police started manhandling the protestors," he says, "and I dove in with the wide-angle lens." Schiappa was ordered away from that spot, and complied, but quickly moved to another.

"If they tell you to get lost," Schiappa says, "go to another spot until you get told to get lost again."

Doug Mills covers the White House, politics, and a lot of major sporting events for the AP.

Every day, he pushes himself, no matter what the assignment, to try for a different picture. "You've got to have the spirit that it will work," he says. "You've got to put

AP photographer Eric Draper had to fight the distraction of police ordering photographers to leave when he spotted an Albanian refugee and his child on a bus in Petrovec, Macedonia, in 1999. Draper was able to make only a few frames.

yourself in the frame of mind to keep trying."

Sometimes that extra work pays off, sometimes it doesn't.

"If you want to make an image no one else has, you have to be willing to take a chance," Mills says. He keeps a mental scorecard and he pushes himself by knowing that taking a chance has paid off a whole lot more than it has failed. "This one didn't work out," he'll say, "but I've paid my dues and next time it will work."

To make this picture of Muhammad Ali with the Olympic torch at the 1996 Games in Atlanta, AP photographer Doug Mills first had to convince security guards and ushers he should be allowed in a position that had been declared off limits.

There are two good examples of it paying off, both by Mills, but each from different situations. The only thing that links them is that Mills took a chance in each instance and it paid off.

• At the Olympic Games in Atlanta in 1996, Mills was assigned to the Opening Ceremonies and his particular assignment was to make a picture of the Olympic torch being lit as part of the festivities. The final torch carrier had been kept a secret.

Even the details of how it would happen were kept hazy.

Mills went to the stadium hours early to get a head start on what he knew would be a crowded situation.

Organizers had issued photographers tickets for a particular area, but Mills quickly figured out that a better picture could be made from across the aisle. A series of conversations with various ushers and security personnel, some contentious at times, finally paid off, and they said Mills could use the spot he had scouted.

But not wanting to tip his hand to the other photographers, he had to hide out first. "I hid above the last row of seats," Mills explained, "on a grate over a big exhaust fan. I couldn't see most of the show and I waited and waited for the right moment."

Several times during those hours of waiting, Mills questioned himself on whether he was doing the right thing. "I just tried to stick to my hunch," he said, "thinking that even if it didn't work out perfectly I'm still going to have a different picture."

Mills' spot was directly between the arena track and the location where the ceremonial flame would be lit. He knew whoever carried the torch would have to pass him. He kept thinking, the cauldron "is above my head, not theirs (the other photographers). Whatever happens has to come past me."

When that moment came, Mills moved into the spot he wanted, but another guard told him he wasn't allowed there. Mills pleaded his case and finally got the word he could stay. Moments later, the gamble paid off and a very fragile Muhammad Ali moved toward that spot with the torch and Mills was able to make two or three frames.

• Sticking to his spot paid off for Mills in another venue, the White House.

What started as an ordinary assignment took on an air of mystery when the meeting was started by Hillary Rodham Clinton without the president there. Normally, everyone waits on him to start. Mills immediately wondered if there was a crisis brewing or if some other news was going on that had detained him.

It was so out of the ordinary that Mills worked his way around to an aisle, normally off limits, to make a picture of Mrs. Clinton speaking, since that could turn out to be a good illustration for the story.

Mills thought to himself, "Until they tell

me to get off the carpet, I'm going to stay here."

Just then, out of the corner of his eye, he spotted a member of the president's security detail in the hallway. And, a moment later, he spotted the president peeking around the corner into the room.

"I glanced over and there he was," Mills said, "standing three feet from me and he didn't say a word or acknowledge that I

After moving from the camera platform to make a different picture of First Lady Hillary Rodham Clinton, Doug Mills of the AP saw President Bill Clinton peeking into the room.

was there. I lifted my camera and an aide, who was standing nearby, signaled to me not to make a picture. I figured, what are they going to do, yell at me?"

Mills made some pictures and the president soon walked past him and took his spot at the head table. Mills had his different picture and taking the chance had put one up on his scorecard's win column.

After all, he says, "if you stick with the pack, you might as well be a potted plant. You're going to take a bunch of average

Reacting to his instincts paid off for AP's Bob Daugherty during a 1979 visit by then-President Jimmy Carter to Bardstown, Ky. During a parade, Carter got out of his car to work the crowd and Daugherty decided against wading into the crowd. Instead, he held his spot on the photo truck and was rewarded when Carter thrilled the crowd by climbing onto the hood.

pictures with a bunch of average guys."

Years earlier, while covering a visit by then-President Jimmy Carter to Bardstown, Ky., Daugherty fought off the urge to wade into the crowd and a few minutes later made a classic campaign picture from the photo truck.

Daugherty says it had been a bad day on the road. No good chances to make any pictures. And it looked like it was getting worse. A few blocks into the parade, Carter got out of his car, Daugherty says, but "his back was to us. My first instinct was to jump the truck. Try to get into the crowd

and get close. But I stayed the course, I stayed on the truck."

Carter quickly got back in the car, traveled a short distance, then got back out of the car. "He got out and hopped on the hood of the car," Daugherty said, and the photo truck was in the perfect position to make a clean picture as the crowd reacted.

"It was not until then that I realized that I had made the right decision to stay with the truck," he says. "Sometimes you have to give up one chance, and then you get a better one if you stay with your plan."

Daugherty says actually making the picture was "very simple. I chose one camera and one lens, an 85 mm. It gave me some atmosphere, and it gave me the speed to overcome some bad light." The picture is one of Daugherty's favorites.

Reinke says any job is going to go better if you're prepared. "The people who plan best from the get-go make the most out of the situation. I can't think of a situation that planning is not going to improve your chances."

"Pictures of tornadoes, for example, are made by people who have film in their camera. That's no time to be trying to load. A fire, a convention, I really can't think of a single situation," Reinke says, "where planning won't pay off. Not one. Sometimes you have to alter those plans but you're in a much better position to alter a plan you have already than when you have no plan at all."

Preparation is an everyday thing, he says. You never know when you're going to have to hit the ground running. He checks his gear quickly every day. "I never leave gear in the car or in the office, so I handle it at least four times every day, at least from my house to the car, and from the car to the office, and back again. I'm always checking straps for wear, and the general condition of the gear."

Reinke says something as simple as having adequate batteries for an assignment can be the difference between success and failure. "I always have a spare ni-cad in my bag. I always have a set of fresh AA batter-

ies in my bag. I figure I can't do much without a functioning camera."

Reinke says he often is asked by a less-prepared photographer if he has any spare batteries, He is quick to reply, "Yes, I do. And they are all charged." But he's less inclined to share. It's a sore point for him

Being alert paid off for AP photographer Marty Lederhandler when, while heading to an assignment in 1994, he spotted several sidewalk Santas coming to the aid of a bicyclist who had been struck by a van on a busy Manhattan street.

and he has little patience for someone who isn't prepared, too.

Feeling comfortable with your equipment is also important, Reinke says. A few years ago, as digital camera technology was changing, Reinke was given a new camera on the eve of the Super Bowl. Promises of better technical quality for his images, and a more responsive camera, were enough for him to use it. He regrets that decision now and vows never to make that mistake again.

"I will never forgive going to a Super Bowl and having a brand new camera in my hands that I had never touched," Reinke says. He had violated one of his own rules on being prepared, this time by not feeling comfortable with his camera. "I might as well have gone out there with a Kodak Instamatic. I know better than that. At least now I do."

That daily preparation should include reading the newspaper to know what is

store. He set the scene in his mind -- "A man is in the store. He has a hostage." He then looked at the options -- "Police could storm the building. He could surrender. He could come out shooting. He could come out with the hostage. He could kill himself in the store."

AP's David Longstreath got his equipment ready, including setting up his long lens on a tripod, and stayed alert as a two-hour Oklahoma City hostage situation unwound.

going on in the world, and your community. Not just the sports pages, but the local section so you'll know the topics and people if you're sent to the city council meeting.

Longstreath, after covering several news events, came up with a mental game he plays. It's called "What if?" It's a scenario development exercise he runs through to help him make order out of chaos at a news scene. It helps him calculate his options.

"As the years go by, you add experiences to your data bank. It's kind of a mental game you play where you try to anticipate what is going to happen."

Longstreath used the exercise while covering a hostage situation in a convenience

By studying the situation, Longstreath was getting his game plan in hand and deciding how to cut down on the chances of missing something. He ran through a list in his mind and then told himself to get a long lens ready. "I better use this lens. If this thing gets going, the adrenaline will be pumping, so get a tripod." He took that precaution so his pictures would be rock steady despite the excitement.

And, he wanted to have long glass to use without being burdened by it if he needed to move quickly. With the lens on a tripod, he could leave it easily and move with the situation. "If I needed to move fast and use a short lens," he said, "I wouldn't want to carry it (the long lens)."

He got himself ready, "set up the f-stop and shutter speed to allow for motion and for depth, put in a fresh roll of film, and waited."

"Two hours later, the gunman ran out the door," Longstreath remembers, "and I pulled closer to the camera, hitting the but-

"and simply say I am open to capturing whatever happens in front of me. Every journalist needs to go to a scene, an event, a happening, and take back the essence of what was there."

"I think there is a difference between anticipation and preconceived notion," he

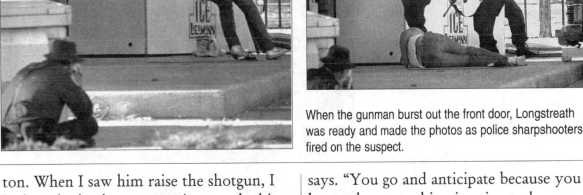

When the gunman burst out the front door, Longstreath was ready and made the photos as police sharpshooters fired on the suspect.

ton. When I saw him raise the shotgun, I had no doubt they were going to take him out." As Longstreath watched and kept making pictures, "the police shot him. At four frames a second, I got 19 frames of him before he hit the ground." The whole incident had come to an end in a few seconds.

Longstreath's thought and preparation put him in the position to make dramatic pictures of the brief, but violent scene. The "what if" exercise had paid off. And, because of this situation, he has more information for his "data bank."

DuCille thinks you should be open-minded in sizing up a scene.

"I try to clear my mind," DuCille says,

says. "You go and anticipate because you know that something is going to happen. You put yourself in a place where you think it will happen. Anticipation is the key word."

However, DuCille warns, "If you go in with preconceived notions, you are going to bring back pictures that are all about you and what was in your head."

"That's why stereotypes flourish," he says, giving an example. "You show up in the black community with a camera. You are looking around for kids spraying in the fountain in the summer. You are stuck with stereotypical images that say 'ghetto' when there could be a thousand other things that can be said if you had only opened your eyes to look and see what is going on."

DuCille says Tom Hardin, who was the director of photography at DuCille's first newspaper job in Louisville, summed it up well. Hardin, DuCille says, told him "photography is 90% anticipation and 10% pressing the button at the right time."

DuCille says he has always followed that as a guide.

Like the instinct for news, experience is the best teacher. Longstreath says those first times at an accident scene or other news events are tough. They're crying. Their child is on the ground. There is only one way to learn how to deal with that, and that is "to be there."

While based in Oklahoma City, Longstreath was tested on that toughness. And, he was tested on two fronts. One was how he would cope with the event. The other was how he would cope with having his efforts overshadowed by the work of another photographer.

Within minutes of the explosion of the federal building there, he was on the scene. "I got there about 15 minutes after the blast."

"The first thing I saw, my first visual memory of that day, was blood in the gutter," he remembers, "and I thought 'This is going to be bad.'" Longstreath made his photos of the victims and the collapsed building, then raced to a working telephone to transmit.

Later, a local amateur photographer, Charles Porter, came into the office with the picture of a fireman carrying a baby. That picture would become the icon of the

As photographer David Longstreath of the AP approached the scene of the federal building bombing in Oklahoma City in 1995, the first thing he saw was blood in the gutter and he knew "this is going to be bad." Over the next several minutes he made pictures of the worst domestic terrorism in U.S. history and then broke away to transmit his images to the world.

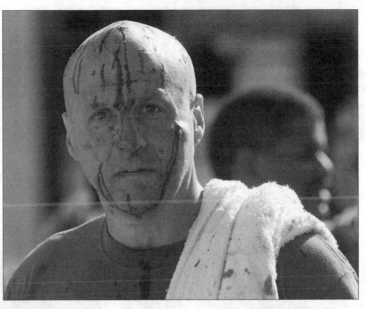

picture," he says. "It could have happened before I got there. It could have happened after I got there. If it had been there and I had been there, I would have made it."

Longstreath says, "I had to let it go at that point," and he kept working the story for the next several months. "The thing that ran through my mind at the end of the day was that I went up that street and into the insanity. I stepped over torsos and limbs and everything else. I did the best possible job I could have

event and Longstreath's efforts, while heroic, would be overshadowed.

That can be tough to swallow. But Longstreath was proud of what he had done and did not feel that his efforts had been diminished.

"I was at that corner. I never saw that

with what I saw. I had to let it go."

Longstreath has reconciled that one aspect but he says he'll never forget what he saw that day. "It's never very far from the surface," he says. "Every April it is a sad day when I remember where I was and what I was doing and the people who died.

A miner relaxes with a cigarette before telling waiting relatives that several miners had been killed in an explosion. For this picture, AP photographer Rusty Kennedy used a long lens so he wouldn't intrude on the private moment.

Everything changed for me April 19, 1995."

Another kind of pressure is the need to be sensitive to your subjects.

AP photographer Rusty Kennedy tells of photographing a coal miner resting for a moment after finding others dead in an explosion. The miner, who had gone into the mine with a rescue team, was gathering his thoughts before telling the families of the trapped men that the miners had been killed. It was a quiet moment. Kennedy explains, "I made the picture with a long lens from some distance. I didn't have to intrude on him. I was able to make it, but he was never aware of me."

"Photographers sometimes get a bad name," Kennedy says, "and we earn it. Sometimes it's a real ugly scene when we intrude."

Even when it's not a sensitive situation like a funeral or accident, photographers can intrude on a subject's personal space. It can be during the arrival of a celebrity at an opening, or a famous personality going home from the hospital, or someone on trial leaving a courthouse.

"Too often, we have that 24 mm lens on the camera," Larry Nighswander of the Ohio University School of Visual Communication says, "and we've got to get in tight. I don't think we do it intentionally to intrude on people, but I know if I do that I'll have a dominant foreground. But, sometimes you have to think, is that worth intruding for?"

Nighswander thinks the number of people covering an event can affect how close a photographer will approach a subject. Sometimes, he says, "if you are going to have one large turnout, you're afraid you'll get blocked, so everyone goes wide and gets in tight."

From outside the pack, "all you see is a sea of photographers. If we could all back up a few steps and make some room, we could use a 105 mm lens and get a better picture." Nighswander doesn't see that happening soon, though. "We're all insecure and we're all afraid we're going to get beat," he says, so the wide-angle lenses stay on the cameras.

Daugherty questions what he calls "driveway journalism," staking out a newsmaker's house.

He's concerned that the presence of photographers and other news people at a subject's home is an unfair pressure on the person's family. "They aren't accused of anything, but unfortunately, when you show up at a man's house, an innocent man until proven guilty, never mind what it might do

to the man, think what it does to his family in the community. That's where I have a little problem. I'm not shy, but it doesn't take much to put yourself in his place. It could be me. You are in front of one family's home creating an atmosphere that doesn't normally exist there."

Reinke says he's changed over the years. Coverage of a bus crash, and the aftermath

Bob Daugherty of the AP calls this "driveway journalism," staking out a person's home or office when they are in the news with no regard to guilt or innocence. In this picture by photographer Juana Anderson, suspected spy Felix Bloch is surrounded by photographers and newspeople in a park near his Washington home.

of the accident that killed two dozen youngsters, was tough for him. "When you have two kids of your own, a story like that begins to wear on you."

"In the beginning it was a great deal easier," Reinke said of his early days in the business. "When my camera was in front of my eye, I was going to squeeze the button until somebody stopped me or I had enough." That's changed for him though. "I think that my tendency now is to not

Sitting near a rose she placed on a Long Island beach, a woman mourns the loss of friends who were crew members on a TWA plane that crashed in 1996. AP photographer Mark Lennihan used a long lens so he wouldn't disturb the woman.

invade privacy as much as I once might have.

"I really felt grieved out at the end of it [the bus crash coverage]. A full week of cemeteries, churches and funeral homes, and so much mourning. I had come to the end of my line on what I could take," he says. "The answer is to take a few days off and hold my own kids and think about how fortunate I am. That helps. Still, I think that grief is one of the most difficult things to photograph," Reinke says, "and each photographer has to draw their own personal lines on what space they will tread on and where they'll stop. Should I have or not? You need to make those decisions on your own."

While covering a mining disaster in eastern Kentucky, Reinke talked quietly with the trapped miners' families at the scene. "It was a case of getting to know the families," he said. Reinke had worked to secure their trust by being open with them, asking when he could make pictures, and being helpful when they needed a hand with something. Later, they invited him into their homes, to the church services and to the burials.

And, even after he had gained their trust, Reinke still was respectful of their situation and made pictures in their homes and at the funerals only when the families felt com-

Knowing when to make a picture and when not to is as important as knowing the mechanical aspects of the craft. While covering the vigil for trapped miners in the mountains of Kentucky, and the subsequent funerals when rescue attempts proved to be futile, AP photographer Ed Reinke talked with the families and built a trust with them.

fortable with him being there.

Reinke says the decisions come quickly, almost automatically when the scene is unfolding in front of you. "The breaking spot news, like Stanley Foreman's pictures of the kids falling from the fire escape," are handled by instinct. "He didn't have any choice but to make those pictures. You make them because it is happening so fast, you don't have time to think about it."

The tough decisions, Reinke says, are "the ones you have to sort out in your mind."

Features and Portraits:
Seeing the World Around Us

Features.

Seeing something that others don't see. Bringing a slice of life to the readers. Making something special out of the ordinary. Something close to the news, but with a twist to it.

Sometimes it can be a single picture. Something from down the street shown in an interesting way. Something that makes you chuckle.

Other times, a feature can be a package of photos. A look at a troublesome situation in your town or on the other side of the world. It can bring a topic worth studying or something more whimsical into your home.

And, portraits.

A straight headshot, almost passport style in presentation. Or a more complex picture such as an environmental portrait, a picture showing something about the person's life or work. Both types of photography bring a different look to a newspaper filled with news and sports pictures.

Ed Reinke calls feature photography "seeing the world around us." Reinke, who is one of those photographers who can go out and bring a good feature home when others struggle, says, "I'm not sure it's an insight into life. It's that I'm willing to watch things unfold."

Reinke is patient. "I'm willing to wait three or four hours to make a good picture of a mundane scene. With planning and

Opposite page: Robert Bukaty saw a notice about the annual Milbridge Days in the Maine town and tucked it away. Months later he pulled it out and checked out the 1999 cod fish relays, where teams dress in foul weather fishing gear and carry a 20-pound fish over a 30-yard course. What resulted was a keeper of a photo for Bukaty.

patience, you can make a silk purse out of a sow's ear." Or at least a humorous picture of some hogs cooling off in a mud hole to go with the day's weather story.

David Longstreath, from his location in

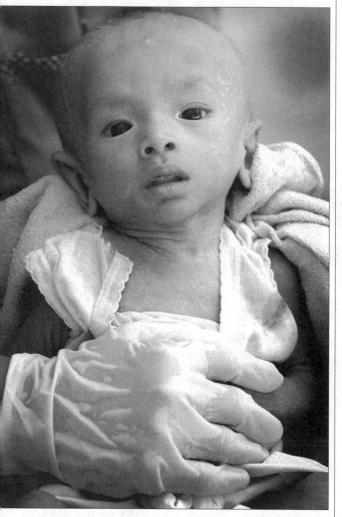

Among the essays AP photographer David Longstreath produces from his base in Bangkok are some based on the tougher side of life. This photo of a Cambodian child, infected with the HIV virus and abandoned at birth, is from an essay Longstreath did in 1999 at a facility in Phnom Penh.

Bangkok, often does feature packages on topics that aren't so pleasant. But, they are important stories that need to be told.

Other times, he works on stories that aren't so harsh but are just as informative — a travel piece on Vietnam, or Cambodia 25 years after the end of the Khmer Rouge regime.

Either kind brings to readers a different part of the world.

"The best ones seem to be the ones you never thought would be out there," Amy Sancetta says. In her role as a national photographer for the Associated Press, Sancetta sometimes takes a look at the lighter side. Other times she handles essays on more serious topics like child labor.

It does seem strange at times to her to make that kind of switch. "In some ways it does seem a little surreal," she says. "You are out in a field with a 6-year-old picking beans when two days before I was at a yo-yo factory. You need to be able to pretty quickly change gears and lock into your subject."

But, she says, if you keep your aim on the human aspect, which is really what it is all about, it will work. "It is all about people," Sancetta says. "You are moving from one situation where you show your humanity to another situation where you do."

Longstreath looks around when he is on news assignments. He tries to find a picture that is away from the hard news situation but that still is a good image that can be tied to a story. "You give them the bread and butter," he says. "But at some point you have to look beyond that."

His photo of a young street urchin in Calcutta is just that kind of picture. While covering the funeral of Mother Teresa,

Longstreath spotted the young boy making his way to the church where the viewing was being held.

India is "one of the most difficult places I have ever worked," Longstreath says. "But also one of the most visually stimulating. The colors, the smells, the sounds, the people. It really comes at you at 300 miles-per-hour."

That's what makes his picture of the young boy so special. Generally, he says, anytime you raise your camera you draw a crowd. But just for a moment that day, Longstreath was able to isolate the youngster who had caught his eye. The picture is better because of its simplicity. The readers' eyes lock into the eyes of the youngster.

"There was a mist that was falling early in the morning. He was just there. He

The sights and sounds come at you at 300 mph in India, says photographer David Longstreath of the AP. But, for just a moment while covering the funeral of Mother Teresa in Calcutta, Longstreath was able to isolate the mourning street urchin with his handful of flowers.

looked lost. It was obvious," Longstreath says, "he wanted to go pay his respects. He had this small bouquet of flowers."

Longstreath says anyone can look at the young man and know, "while he may be poor and desperate, he is still a human being. It was his feeling that this person (Mother Teresa) was very important to him. You have to see it through his eyes, too."

It happened quickly. "I don't remember shooting more

A feature picture with a good story peg. Just what a lot of picture editors are asking for. AP photographer Mark Duncan silhouetted a bridge engineer against the backdrop of Cleveland's Terminal Tower as she practiced her climbing techniques with colleagues.

that catches you."

Reinke, who has a knack for slice-of-life features, says photographers should make feature pictures that people can relate to, so they'll say, "I remember when I did that when I was a kid."

"Feature pictures really elicit a response from the public. You have to realize that most people never get their picture in the newspaper, and when they do, a good percentage would rather not," he says. "When we can

than two frames. That was all I needed. There was no reason to work the situation any harder. When I saw it through the viewfinder, I knew it was the moment I needed."

Those subtle moments are the difficult ones to catch, but the ones that really pay off, he says. "Photographing out-of-control emotion," like at a funeral or disaster, "is easy to do. The subtle emotion is the one

go out and make pleasant pictures of people doing things that are interesting, it's a plus for the people we serve."

But Alex Burrows isn't so sure of the light, stand-alone feature picture's place in the newspaper. "Newspapers should try to get away from stand-alones and make pictures pair up with stories more," he says.

Editors at his newspaper, *The Virginian-Pilot* in Norfolk, "have come to the conclusion that this is not what we want to do," he says. "We want to have pictures run with stories." Burrows' paper "rarely has one on the cover," and if it plays a stand-alone feature at all, "it's usually inside."

When Larry Nighswander was the picture editor at *The Cincinnati Post,* the staff called feature pictures "the citizen of the day."

"They like to take an average Joe and make him a star for the day," he says. "Something funny, outlandish, a juxtaposition, a relationship or a lifestyle that people aren't aware of. You're giving a reader a chance to be a star for the day. Those are the ones that people cut out and put on their refrigerator, not the news picture but the quiet feature. People like to step back and just enjoy their community."

But J. Bruce Baumann of the Evansville, Ind., *Courier and Press* says, "It just can't be a pretty picture. They really don't have any place in newspapers. That's not to say there aren't good feature pictures to run," he says, "but they need to express some kind of information that is useful."

"There are so many things that can be photographed that are connected with real life events in the community," Baumann says. "Kids jumping over sprinklers or dogs with funny sunglasses create a credibility problem. How can someone (the photographer) be taken seriously?"

Reinke's picture of a farmer painting his barn in rural Kentucky showed a typical country scene, a chance to step back and enjoy. The photo was made interesting by the choice of angles and lenses. But, it didn't just happen.

He says he found it the way he finds 90 percent of his feature pictures. "I was driving down a road and saw a new barn with a ladder, but there was no one around. I knew someone was going to paint that

Picture editors debate the usefulness of standalone feature pictures. AP photographer Ed Reinke, who has a knack for the slice-of-life look at the lighter side of our world, thinks they have a place and saw this scene while driving near his home in rural Kentucky.

barn, so I went on 15-20 miles and had an iced tea. Then I came back down the road and the farmer was painting."

Reinke talked to the farmer about his new barn, got the man comfortable with him being there and "about two hours later I made the picture just the way I wanted it."

Baumann thinks that may not be a good investment of time. "Rarely will a photographer just 'find' a picture. That kind of aimless, directionless photography doesn't have a place." When you look at salaries and car expenses, Baumann says, "it's a waste of resources to have them go out there without any direction." He says photographers should find a good topic, research it, then shoot it. "That offers a lot more opportunity for pictures with content."

raphers' resources."

"It is all in the planning," he says.

To help with that planning, the *Free Press* picture desk maintains a tickler file of events that are coming up, and on slow days, they can dip into that file to come up with an idea that at least has some peg to an event of community interest.

While at a Bath, Maine, shipyard on another story, AP photographer Robert Bukaty made this striking photo of a worker dwarfed by a ship's screw. Bukaty made the picture and pegged it to the ship's launching later in the week. A good eye for an interesting angle and the right choice of lenses gave the picture drama. The news peg earned it space in newspapers looking for a feature with a purpose.

Or, they try to think of something firm to work on instead of just cruising. "You've got to go out and do a weather picture," he says, if that is the news of the day. But on a blistering hot day instead of heading for a swimming pool, he says, "How about something on the hottest job in the city? Working on a tar crew on the street or in a hotel laundry. It is the kind of picture that has to have information, has to have a purpose."

Rob Kozloff of the Detroit *Free Press* agrees with Baumann. "It trivializes what the photographers are doing for the paper," he says. "That may be a little harsh but I think it is true. They are journalists, too, out gathering information for the readers."

"I want everything in the paper to have importance. To have a reason to be there," Kozloff says. "I don't want it just to be a found situation. That is a waste of photog-

Reinke thinks there is a place for feature pictures without always having a news peg. "I don't think pictures have to be prize winners to be good. Making pictures for that day's edition is what we are paid to do, a nice picture on a slow day."

Jeanne Mell, the director of photography at the Wilmington, Del., *News-Journal,* agrees with Reinke that those "slice of life" pictures have a place. "I really enjoy the fact that some of the newspaper's photographers can come back with something you hadn't planned on to really make the paper zing."

"I think the paper would be really boring if we didn't have stand-alone features," she says. "Features are a good way to reflect the community." And, a way to "get people into the paper who would not normally be part of it."

Rusty Kennedy also enjoys features, but he especially likes long-term projects that have some depth, the kind of feature photography that Burrows and Baumann advocate.

Kennedy once spent "a couple of months, maybe ten hours a week," visiting a group of homeless shelters and photographing the people who lived in them. Kennedy says the project started almost by accident. "I was down in that area on another assignment and saw the people sitting outside. They shouted to me to 'take my picture' and I started to talk to them. They were interesting people. I started going down there, started wandering around."

The project, which was shot several years ago, was an early glimpse at a growing national problem. "They were homeless," Kennedy says, "before people really talked

For a 1974 series of portraits of the homeless in Philadelphia, AP's Rusty Kennedy worked on the essay as time permitted. The result was striking photos including this one of an older man with his dinner, a bowl of soup.

about that."

Kennedy brought pictures with him each time he visited, but "they never were really interested in seeing the pictures. More the attention of me having interest in them." That project "made ten good pictures. That was one of the favorite things that I've done. It had some depth. So much

Changing gears
Covering the full spectrum of childhood

One day, she's photographing the struggle of children working to help support their families. A few days later, she is making pictures of youngsters preparing for a recital or taking part in an Easter egg hunt.

Amy Sancetta says, "You do need to pretty quickly be able to change gears and lock into your subject."

But she finds that change of pace isn't difficult for her. "Shifting gears isn't all that hard for me because it is all about people. You're moving from one situation where you show your humanity to another situation where you do."

of what we do is for the moment."

Eric Risberg also prefers the feature package.

Risberg uses much of his time preparing himself for the assignment. "I approach them with lots of research. I'll go out, spend a day, try to find out everything I can about the subject. And I'll keep going back after the initial shoot to fill in any gaps." Risberg tries "taking a second, or a third, or a fourth look at things" to round out his stories.

He used this approach for a package on bike messengers. "It started out where I just hung out at the office and saw them dispatched, taking that time to understand the operation, meet people. Then another day I actually did the job. I got on a mountain bike and rode with the messenger and I got to see the little alleys and streets."

"It was a success because I was involved," Risberg says, "and that also is true of the sailing package," a set of photographs on a San Francisco-area entry in the America's Cup competition. For that package, Risberg sailed with the crew four times, including one sail where he worked as a grinder on the boat. "I didn't make any pictures that first day, I just took notes and did what they do, and came up with ideas."

Risberg went back out again three times, making pictures on those trips. "For that package I wanted a unique view of what they were doing, the boat and the men."

Risberg wanted one picture that captured the whole story. "I thought I could do that by putting a camera on top of the mast looking down, but I couldn't get it to work. So, I agreed to be at some risk, and I

was hoisted up to the top in a bosun's chair."

Risberg had one hand on a guide wire and one hand on a camera, but despite the danger, he thought it was more than worth it. "That picture summed it up. It showed you a different view of the boat, and got

Near the top of the mast, Eric Risberg of the AP hung on to a safety line with one hand while holding his camera with the other to make this 1986 picture of a racing yacht.

the point across about all of the men it takes to run a boat like this and the teamwork involved."

Essays may be done on many topics. Essays can even be done on different

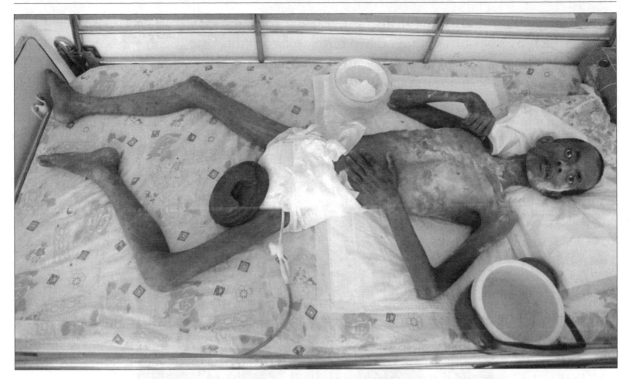

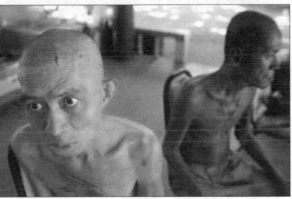

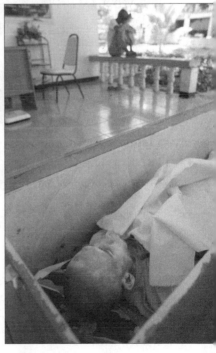

aspects of a single subject.

A hospice for AIDS victims in northern Thailand was Longstrcath's first picture package after he transferred to Bangkok from a post in Oklahoma City.

Longstreath heard about the hospice and checked the bureau's files to see what had been done on it. "They had done this particular hospice before," Longstreath says, "but the pictures were more of the monks who ran the place, not something central to an individual patient there." It was a troublesome story. "Once they got to the hospice, there was no hope left."

He spent the first couple of days at the hospice gathering impressions without making pictures. After that visit, Longstreath says, "I wrote a lot of my thoughts, my impressions. I spent the longest time thinking about this."

That helped him clarify the theme of the story, which he not only photographed but also wrote. "When I went back to photograph it," he says, "I had not a shopping list but a clearer idea of what it was like, what I was seeing."

Longstreath ended up shooting for two days. "I remember thinking I needed to shoot more," he says, "but then I went through the film and realized that I had what I needed."

Not all feature assignments are shot over a long period of time, or have an exotic dateline. There are the daily needs to fill, like Reinke's barn painter, and others. Even then, a little thought goes a long way.

Sancetta says it's sometimes easier to have an idea in the back of your head, even when cruising for a daily feature. "I try to have something out there to

You can't help but smile when you look at this feature picture by Paul Sakuma of the AP. Arriving early for a 1993 sumo tournament in San Jose, Calif., Sakuma captured the mock battle between the youngster and a wrestler weighing more than 500 pounds.

aim for," she says. "When I do go out, I try to have spots that I head for — a park, a pool. Once I looked up in the phone book a place that makes ice to make a feature to match the hot weather story."

"You can drive around and never find anything," she warns. "It's nice to have some goals, or you'll find yourself really frustrated."

For her multi-picture feature projects, Sancetta keeps a running list of ideas she has gotten from a variety of places. "Part of it is just being interested in things," Sancetta says. "If I ever think of anything, I write it down. Or if I see something in a book or magazine that sets off an idea, I make a note of it."

Sancetta has been doing these feature packages for several years and says the hardest part is coming up with the idea.

"But I just came up with another list with thirty new things," she says. "Some will work out. Some won't. Some I'll do. Some I won't end up doing."

One example of Sancetta's work is a look at the man who invented the pink flamingo lawn ornament.

Sancetta read a one-paragraph story, "a tiny blurb," about the company in an in-flight magazine while traveling to another assignment. The story had only a single picture of the owners, but it piqued her interest.

"I called them up," she says, and arranged to go to the factory to meet with the owner and his wife. "I went out and talked to them, saw how they make them, and heard his story." The story "just kind of grew from there."

The key picture in the essay was of the owner surrounded by his products. An off-beat portrait of sorts. Sancetta says she was able to make that picture by developing a good rapport with him. "The reason I was able to get Don Featherstone to climb into this enclosed area and be covered by pink flamingoes was because we had such a great day together," she says. "We really hit it

off. He was a really wacky guy. He was game for it!"

Another picture story of Sancetta's was on a Vermont summer camp for dogs and their owners. She calls the pictures and text she wrote, "one of the silliest stories I ever did."

These two examples turned into fun looks at some not-very-serious topics, but Sancetta got back a stack of clips from each package. "I got back dozens and dozens of full-page clips from around the country," she says. Different papers used different combinations of the story and pictures, but "it got used again and again and again."

"There is a place for all of it," she says. "Newspapers are doing everything they can to keep the readership interested," and Sancetta thinks that these light-hearted features help balance the bad news that is part of our world every day.

While Sancetta does lots of research, when she can, on many of her topics, she also likes to go with the flow as she makes her pictures. "You have to think about your story," she says. "How you are going to go at it. But you have to be open to

AP photographer Amy Sancetta surrounded Don Featherstone, the creator of the pink flamingo lawn ornament, with his favorite product for a whimsical 1998 portrait. Featherstone created the pink American icon as a young designer fresh out of college more than 40 years ago.

what's going on around you. You have to leave yourself open for things that you can't anticipate."

"Part of shooting a story is being surprised yourself," Sancetta says. But she also says you'll have a better chance of winning a subject's trust if you can show that you've got some knowledge of who they are and what they do. "You need to be able to roll with the changes," she says, "but you should know something about your subject. You should find some way to relate to your topic that shows your subject you are interested in them. That just makes them want to share with you more." And the payoff is often times like that flamingo portrait of hers.

Jerome Delay of the AP's Paris staff warns that you have to be open to whatever happens. "Don't go in with a list of photographs," he says. "You must not control the situation but you do need to put yourself in the situation." Patience, he says, is the key.

AP photographer George Widman agrees with Sancetta that you need to have some idea of where you want to end up. He says his feature hunts are "a mix, cruising and something on my mind. It's a lot harder to find a feature when you have nothing on your mind." Widman says he also tries to think of a peg -- "What's the weather? What's the news? It's not always easy to make a feature that has any relevance."

But his picture of a homeless man standing over a steaming grate to keep warm a few days after Christmas was extremely relevant. "The key is the date," Widman says. "Campaigns for the homeless always stop

after Christmas."

He remembers "it was a really cold day, and these guys are still there. They didn't go away with the Christmas wrappings." Widman made a picture of one man and "I talked with him, tried to get him to go to a

Coming on the heels of the Christmas season, this portrait of a Philadelphia homeless man keeping warm over a steam grate drew a lot of interest. George Widman of the AP photographed the man, then tried to talk him into going to a shelter on a very cold day.

shelter, but he refused." Widman said it was a tough shoot. "I used a 180 mm, at a 60th wide open, and I was shaking because it was so cold."

But the picture worked and was widely displayed. "It was very early morning light, gold light, and the business person walking by in the background put it all together for me."

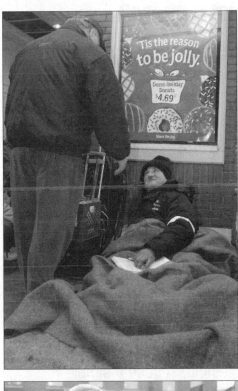

Elise Amendola of the AP's Boston bureau photographed an annual event, a census of homeless people in the city during the Christmas holidays, but it turned out to be a better story

than usual when the estranged brother of a man in her pictures came forward and sought her help in locating his homeless sibling.

Sometimes a simple feature assignment turns into a good news story, too.

An annual event in Boston involves the mayor going around with workers taking a census of homeless people. AP photographer Elise Amendola had done the assignment before when it popped up again on a cold December day.

This one turned out a little differently, though.

While making the rounds with the mayor, Amendola photographed a homeless person in front of a festive Christmas sign. She put out that one and two others. It seemed like a pretty routine assignment. The next morning, a newspaper in the

Boston suburbs, the *Worcester Telegram*, ran the picture of the man in front of the sign.

Amendola got a call in the office from a *Telegram* reader. He told her that the man in the picture was a long lost brother. "Can you help me find him?" he asked. They arranged to meet the next night. Amendola took him to where she had made the picture but the man wasn't there. After asking other men in the area, it didn't take long to find him. "We found him within 45 minutes," she says.

The homeless man didn't recognize his brother for a couple of seconds. But, when he did, they hugged, and it was an emotional scene.

Amendola stood a few feet away and made pictures of the reunion. It was "that kind of moment where you have to stay focused and calm," she says. "You are anticipatory, but you must remain dispassionate. You have to do that, or you can't shoot."

She warns, "You can't get caught up in the moment."

The reunion story got wide play and the family had another a few days later with national television there. The intimacy of that first reunion had been lost though. It was, "so much better when it was one on one. So much more real," Amendola says.

Weeks after the Exxon Valdez oil spill in Alaska, John Gaps III was assigned to do a feature on it.

Gaps wanted to make a picture showing the effect of the oil on the fish and vegetation under the surface. He thought back to a picture he'd seen in college of a diver entering the water. It had been made by

My first camera?

Alex Burrows: He had to borrow a camera for college and got his first camera, a Nikon F, after getting out of school. He still has it, displayed in his bathroom at home. The bathroom serves as Burrows' "museum" and has several items from his career.

Larry Nighswander: "My first camera was an Argus C3 bought at a drug store with tip money from delivering the Fostoria Times-Review."

Gary Kemper: "I earned it selling seed packets. When I had sold enough to win something, I chose a simple Kodak box camera."

partially submerging a camera, using a fish tank as a shell.

Gaps thought this might work. "I went to the pet store and bought an aquarium, and carried the thing for four days. I tried it once and it didn't work because there was too much oil. So, a couple of days later I was out on an island and it looked like a better situation. I got down in the water and balanced the aquarium on a rock."

"I had to get the camera as far back as possible from the glass to work," Gaps says, "since the tank's glass worked much like a ground glass in a large-format camera. I was actually shooting the glass." Gaps used a 24 mm lens and made a series of exposures.

Getting a usable density on the film was tough. "It was overcast," he says. "That was a prerequisite for doing it to get the exposure in a usable range. I tilted the camera down for an exposure reading in the water, then up to meter the sky, and I split the difference. It was about a three-stop range." Gaps shot the scene of underwater life and men working on the shore at f16 to get the depth of field he needed.

Even with all of that work, there was some disappointment. "It wasn't exactly what I wanted, but I didn't think it was going to get any better," Gaps says.

Reinke says there are no rules for feature photography when it comes to equipment or film. "It's whatever the situation warrants," he says. As a general rule, Reinke tries to make the picture at the slowest possible film speed, but sometimes he'll use an ASA1600 rating in the fog, "to bring up the contrast and give the picture a certain effect."

Nighswander says that when he was shooting daily, he used long lenses to keep from being spotted. "I found myself using telephotos 80 percent of the time," to control the depth of field for cleaner pictures, and most importantly for obtaining candid pictures. "As soon as the photographer is spotted," Nighswander says, "the spontaneity is gone."

Sancetta agrees you use what you need, and thinks the simple approach is the best. "I try to do things as simply as possible. You can gizmo yourself right out the window."

Reinke explains that "ours is to interpret what we see into a mood or feeling. You have to choose whatever lens and film that allows you to do that."

"Feature photography is a prime way to step back and enjoy life, the quiet moments," says Nighswander. "In our rush to report the news, we sometimes overlook what the reader wants. Every editor in

AP photographer Rusty Kennedy used available light from a nearby window and exposed for the highlights to give texture to a portrait of artist Carolyn Wyeth. A slow shutter speed helped accentuate the wispy cigarette smoke.

America needs to evaluate that."

While features sometimes catch people unaware, the portrait is best made when the photographer and the subject are working together.

Reinke says there's been a big change since he started nearly thirty years ago. "In the early '70s when I started at a newspaper, we didn't want to run pictures of people looking into the camera." He explains that "that's different now. I like to have them look at me right through the camera,

Portraits can take on a variety of looks. Different photographers have different styles and use different techniques. The resulting photographs each draw your eye in different ways. Elise Amendola used sidelighting to highlight the cigar smoke of Boston Celtics executive Red Auerbach (above right). Wyatt Counts sometimes steps back, as in the this portrait of young actress Anna Paquin (above left) while sometimes he uses a wide angle lens and gets in close with his subject like in his portrait of the personal barber to the British royal family (left).

Other times, Counts changes his perspective to bring interest to his portraits as in this photo of actress Nicole Kidman (left). Again varying his style, Counts used a more straight-on approach in a portrait of Alexander Lieberman with paintings he has done (bottom). Amy Sancetta used a globe as a prop and a high perspective to clean up the background and emphasize the size of a youngster whose essay on hopes and dreams ("I will save the world with my super goodness") had been included in a book (below).

to talk to me through the camera, to talk with their hands toward me."

New York freelance photographer Wyatt Counts involves his subjects in making the picture better. "Rather than force a setup on a subject, I try to get them to give me as much input as possible," he says. Often, Counts says, it works best when you end up "assisting" the subject.

For a portrait of artist-author Laurent de Brunhoff, who continues the character Babar the elephant that was created by his father, Counts first thought of getting one of De Brunhoff's books, or a Babar poster, to use as a prop. But he was afraid that might be awkward.

So he brought a pen to the photo session and talked with the artist about what it is like to draw Babar. De Brunhoff then quickly sketched a likeness of Babar on his hand, using the thumb as the trunk.

Counts made a test exposure on Polaroid film and gave it to De Brunhoff, who really liked the photo. Counts had a relaxed subject, and soon had his picture, too.

Sancetta's portrait of a scientist doing research on the effect of light on people's moods is a simple, straightforward picture. But, by using the light available to her, Sancetta made an eye-catching picture.

When she first arrived at the assignment, the scientist had already enlisted the aid of a volunteer to model his invention — a hat with a light built into the rim. Sancetta made a few frames of that setup, with the scientist "helping" the volunteer with the headgear. That would have been the picture to make several years ago. But, Sancetta wanted to more closely tie the scientist to the helmet without the awkward set-up look of the two-person pose.

To show the effect of the light built into the helmet's rim, Sancetta first had the scientist turn on the battery-powered light, then turn off all of the other lights in the room. The result was a well-exposed pic-

To illustrate a story on a scientist studying the effect of light on people's moods, Amy Sancetta of the AP had the man wear the specially rigged helmet. Sancetta made a simple portrait but, by paying attention to the details, also made an excellent illustration for the story.

ture of the scientist's face, but the shape of the safari-type helmet was lost against the dark background.

Sancetta solved that problem by putting the scientist on a stool in an open doorway with all of the hall lights on behind him. The hall lights provided the separation needed to bring out the helmet without losing the effect of the light built into the brim of the hat.

Sancetta also could have provided that separation by lighting the background with a strobe set to put out at least a stop less light than the face was getting from the fluorescent tube. If she had intended to use the picture as a color illustration, she could have also put a gel on the strobe to introduce a color to the background, perhaps balancing it with the fluorescent of the helmet fixture.

But, since the picture was intended primarily for black and white use, the hallway lights were a simple solution that worked well.

"My style is to surround people with the things that distinguish them from other people," Sancetta says. "When you go into someone's environment to shoot a portrait, there is something around the subject that makes them special. Everyone has something that is a symbol of what they do."

To quickly establish a working relationship with the subject, Sancetta simply asks them to explain what they do. She says that gets them talking and relaxed, while at the same time giving herself ideas for pictures.

But, Sancetta makes an important point

AP photographer Robert Bukaty wanted to make a portrait that would reflect the basic elements of the life of young entertainer Slaid Cleaves. He took Cleaves out to the misty parking lot after the late show and perched him on the fender of his well-worn 1974 Dodge Dart.

when she tells of her last step before making the picture. "I trace my eye around the outside of the frame, slowly around the corner to see if it works, or if I've left unwanted dead space. If you do that, it will tell you if the picture is not balanced. I'm really conscious of what space is open and what space has something in it. For instance, if I have an open space on the left, I try to balance it with an open space on the right. You can balance empty space the same way you can balance busy space."

Sometimes you can't move the subject to make a better picture. If the subject can't move, then it's up to the photographer. Sancetta suggests changing your perspective on some assignments to give the reader a different view.

That isn't difficult, she says. "You can lay

For a zany 1999 portrait of Tampa Bay Devil Rays marketing vice president Mike Veeck, AP photographer Eric Gay took a high angle and Veeck reclined on the team's logo on the field. Veeck is the son of famed baseball wizard Bill Veeck, no stranger to crazy stunts to help fill the stands so the offbeat pose went well with the story.

on the ground, you can stand on a table." For a portrait of an organist, Sancetta checked with the subject, then took off her shoes and stood on top of the organ. "I

looked down on him. There must have been 600 keys. It made a nice picture, no dead space. He's surrounded by the keyboard."

"It's a good example of looking for a different angle for a portrait instead of being eye to eye with the subject," she says.

For the most part, none of the pictures required anything fancy. Just a knowledge of how to make light and composition work to the photographer's advantage. And, to give the reader something more interesting to look at.

While Sancetta's picture of the scientist is an interesting illustration, sometimes editors are just looking for a good one-column picture to go with a story.

The simple headshot takes some care, though, to make sure the picture is a good one and can be easily reproduced.

The first item is to find a neutral background, one that won't distract or isn't too dark. A busy background pulls the reader's eye away from the subject. A dark background makes it difficult to separate the subject from the backdrop.

If you're stuck with a busy background, try to bring the subject some distance away from it, and use a wider aperture on your lens to throw the background out of focus.

If you have no alternative to a dark background, use Pizac's method and try lighting the background with a strobe, or moving a nearby lamp into position to give a rim-lit quality to the subject. Fill the subject's face with a strobe set to put out slightly more light than your rear illumination. This will provide the separation you need for good reproduction in the newspaper.

Have the subject sit, if possible. And, have the subject move forward to the edge of the seat, so their shoulders don't sag. Or, have them face you with their arms crossed. That is a relaxing pose for many people.

Then, photograph them from a slight angle to get the most pleasing "look" to the picture.

That front light can be managed to minimize the "flash" look. Use a strobe bounced off a ceiling, and a reflector card or your fingers to "kick" light into the subject's eyes and the shadows of his face.

The best lens for simple portraits is in the 85 mm-105 mm range. This gives a workable image size on 35 mm film without the photographer having to be on top of the subject. It also lets you throw the background out of focus by using the wider apertures.

No matter what kind of a portrait you want, you should first master the basics of the simple headshot. Then, by adding elements, you can make that headshot more sophisticated.

Even Sancetta's picture of the scientist uses the basic rules of the simple headshot to achieve a high level of quality.

Counts says that is important. "My basic thought is to start with the simple picture, then start adding elements," he says. Counts starts tight, then pulls back slowly watching as the elements are added.

You add an element to give the reader some identification with the subject. You

New York freelance photographer Wyatt Counts does a lot of celebrity portraits, often in a sterile hotel room. Counts tries different, sometimes offbeat methods to put some interest in his photos, but he met his match in comedian Bill Murray who assisted in carefully trashing the room in 1996.

haven't really taken away from the simplicity of the basic headshot, only improved on it. You put the subject into a setting that will provide greater identification for the reader. Now you have elevated the simple headshot to an environmental portrait.

If you look closely, the simple headshot is still in there. A clean view of the subject, conceived like a one-column, but deserving of more space. The photographer has made a versatile picture that fills any need.

Sports:
Peak Action and Telling Reaction

Sports photography. Dreams of the Super Bowl, the Olympics and the World Series. But reality is often a high school football game, the college team down the road, or Little League baseball in the summer.

All of those events, from the biggest to the smallest, are important, though, since surveys show a large number of newspaper readers get the paper for the sports section.

Peak action, or telling reaction, is what you strive for. A different picture, if you can. Not just settling for the obvious.

The picture you want is simple, Ed Reinke says. "It is the peak, story-telling action. It's just that simple. There is peak action, then there is the story of the game, but the picture that works best is the one that incorporates both. That's the journalism part of sports photography."

"It's not good enough to make a picture if it doesn't mean anything. There was a time, when I was starting out in the early '70s, when it seemed you could aim your camera at second base and just wait for the play to happen," Reinke says. "Now you're looking for peak action and the picture that tells the story. Sports is no different than news in that the best product we can offer is the perfect marriage of the action and story."

The key is simply paying attention.

Opposite page: Peak action is one of the mainstays of sports photography and AP photographer Dusan Vranic has captured that moment with this picture from the Euro 2000 soccer championships in the Netherlands.

Rusty Kennedy tells of watching a struggling pitcher in action and looking for something odd that might give him a picture in a dull game. Fearing he would miss

don't look for the odd picture. Sometimes newcomers will make a better picture because they aren't locked into that formula journalism."

Preparation is important, Sports Illustrated photographer John Biever says, as is getting to the event early so you can get settled and take a moment to find out what is going on. Biever is known for arriving two to three hours before an event. He says it helps him to relax and size things up. "Some guys walk in during the national anthem," he says, adding "I'd

By not going to his long lens too quickly, freelance photographer Jeff Zelevansky captured the scene and told more of the story of the reaction by players and fans to the 1999 perfect game thrown by New York Yankees pitcher David Cone, kneeling.

something if restricted to the narrow view of the camera, "I watched without having the camera to my face and I spotted his hat falling in front of his eyes when he'd have a hard follow-through. Then I trained the camera on him for a few pitches and caught it," Kennedy says. He had his different picture.

He warns that it's easy to fall into a rut covering baseball, or any sport. "We are sometimes in a formula kind of thing, and

be catching up the whole game and it just wouldn't work for me."

AP's Eric Risberg says you have to fight the pattern of going to a sports event, no matter what it is, and working from habit. He says the best approach "is to not always go to the same place. Try other spots for variety. By moving around a bit, it helps you keep your enthusiasm and interest up because you're looking at it from different perspectives."

Like Kennedy, Reinke likes to watch the pitchers, hoping for something different. And it has worked for him, too. "This was a simple matter of knowing I could commit to staying on a pitcher. I was going to make a picture of the pitcher getting hit by a ball hit back through the middle, and it took two games, but it made a great picture." Mark that one up to patience.

Kennedy credits much of his success at sports photography to using extremely long telephoto lenses (400 mm-800 mm) to isolate his subjects. "I always try to use the longest lens possible," he says. "You have a good expression, and you throw the background out of focus, the subject really jumps out at you."

He says he was using long lenses before they became commonplace. "I was willing to take my chances. It was worth the risk to me of losing a few pictures along the way to use the longest lens possible. I've seen a lot of real good pictures ruined by being under-lensed."

Using the long glass helps Biever achieve the look he wants in his pictures, too. "What I've always tried to do," Biever says, "is shoot as tight as possible and show as much emotion in the faces of the athletes." He says that isn't a novel technique but is a good one he has adapted for his use.

Reinke is a little more conservative in his choice of lenses. "I think it depends on the

coverage. If I'm alone, I will tend to shoot loose enough to not crop something out of the frame that I want, and still blow it up to a good image."

It took Ed Reinke a couple of games of concentrating on the pitcher, but that plan paid off with a good picture of reaction to a line drive.

Lens selection also can be dictated at times by the event and the size of the crew you're working with.

"At a Super Bowl or World Series, the tendency is to be as tight as possible because there is no question that the peak action is enhanced by tightness in the shooting," Reinke says.

"But, when you're alone, you can't afford the risks you can take when you have team coverage," he says.

Even when covering a regular season college basketball game where he has another photographer working with him, his approach is also different. "That makes me feel like I can use a 180 mm at the basket, because I'm covered by the other person. If I'm the only one there, I generally won't take that chance."

John Gaps III was faced with a hard choice like that in the closing moments of the 2000 Super Bowl in Atlanta's Georgia Dome. With the clock winding down, the Tennessee Titans had to score on the next play or lose the Super Bowl. Gaps saw there was a lot going on with the St. Louis Cardinals starting to celebrate and the crowd getting cranked up.

But nothing else was as important to Gaps as making sure that goal line was covered.

"There's no time for heroes then," Gaps says. "You should just cover your zone."

"I had two-thirds of the goal line covered with the 80-200 zoom," he says, "and my wide angle on my second camera in case they dropped down in front of me."

He recognized that this wasn't a time to gamble on a long lens. "It didn't matter about my creative juices," Gaps says. "That was the news."

And Gaps' quick planning paid off. His picture of Titans back Kevin Dyson, reaching in vain for the goal line and falling inches short as the final whistle blew, was on front pages around the world the next morning.

Sports Illustrated picture editor Porter

There were only a few seconds left in the 2000 Super Bowl matchup between the Tennessee Titans and the St. Louis Rams in Atlanta and John Gaps III, then a photographer with the AP, knew Tennessee's only chance for a win would be to score. So he worked his way into a position to protect the goal line and got his equipment in order. He was ready then when Titans running back Kevin Dyson thundered toward the goal line making an unsuccessful last-second lunge.

Binks believes that his choices have evolved. When Binks was just beginning to shoot sports, he thought "you had to shoot everything with a 300, then a 400, then a 600. After making an untold number of mistakes, I learned there was nothing wrong with having a wide-angle lens hanging around your neck. It has helped me, that's for sure."

Every sports fan has a favorite picture.

One of the classics is Harry Cabluck's picture of Boston Red Sox batter Carlton Fisk trying to use body language to keep a home-run ball fair in the sixth game of the 1975 World Series against Cincinnati. Baseball historians call it one of the greatest baseball games ever played, and Cabluck's picture is the symbol of that game.

Cabluck's position was in centerfield, just over the fence with an 800 mm lens. His primary assignment was to shoot every pitch, hoping to get the home runs and key hits from a different perspective.

Cabluck says the assignment called for concentration, some skill and a lot of luck. When shooting, Cabluck says he watched and followed the game, "just like being an outfielder. What am I going to do if the ball is hit to me?" Cabluck was constantly refining what he was going to do in any given situation.

When Fisk swung that bat and danced down that line, Cabluck moved with him, firing frames that tell the story of Fisk's struggle as he watched the ball arc toward foul territory. He then shot the jubilation as the ball stayed fair for the home run.

Despite moments when Fisk was obscured by other players, Cabluck concentrated and stayed with him because he knew that Fisk was the story of that game.

base looks different from those perspectives.

Elise Amendola took a chance on a different perspective at a golf tournament, and an unorthodox lens choice, to make a beautiful picture of Davis Love III winning the

AP photographer Elise Amendola had spent the final day of the 1997 PGA Championship fighting the rain and wind to just keep her cameras in operation when, as she neared the final green with leader Davis Love III, a rainbow appeared. Amendola made the decision then to not concentrate on a tight picture of Love reacting to his win, but to go for the more visual approach with a wide angle view that included the arc over the green.

That kind of coverage can be extended to a Little League or high school baseball game. Instead of taking the safe position along the first base line, try shooting from one of the foul poles, or from just over the centerfield fence. Even a play at second

PGA Championship.

Amendola, and others working with her, had battled pouring rain all day. "We were struggling," she explains. "Just keeping the gear dry was a problem."

But, as she walked with Love, the tourney leader, up the 18th fairway, the skies began to brighten. "Walking toward his approach shot, I saw a rainbow emerging. It was beautiful and I was hoping I could do something with it."

When they got to the green, Amendola knew other members of the AP crew were already there and she had some freedom to take an off-beat position. So she took a spot to Love's back and decided to go with her wide-angle lens, although she noticed other photographers near her were using long lenses.

"There was debate in my mind about what lens to use," she says, "but I said to myself, 'I'm going to go loose and use this rainbow.'"

Amendola said she wasn't sure she had a great picture. She had concerns about the technical quality and whether the picture captured the moment the way she saw it.

Her fears were erased when she got back to the trailer where the AP crew was working and she got a big hug from the other members. "It all came together," she explains. "The winning golfer, winning a major, the rainbow. It all came together so beautifully."

For pure joy, it is hard to beat Dave Martin's picture of 1999 Ryder Cup team captain Ben Crenshaw celebrating after his team's dramatic final-day comeback for the win over the European squad.

An AP photographer, Martin was working at a disadvantage since organizers had limited the number of photo bibs for prime

access at the event and Martin was working without one. That didn't slow Martin down, though; he takes making the picture which shows the joy of victory or the agony of defeat as a personal crusade.

"I am very determined," he says. "I put a

Working without a photographer's identifying vest, Dave Martin of the AP worked his way into a position away from the other photographers and made this wonderful picture of U.S. Ryder Cup team captain Ben Crenshaw celebrating the squad's miracle comeback in the 1999 matches outside Boston.

lot of pressure on myself." Early on in his career, he says, he was told action photographers were a dime a dozen but a photographer who could capture reaction sets himself above the rest of the field.

Martin says he learns from his mistakes — everything from tripping over untied shoelaces to having his aperture get knocked off kilter in a post-game crowd on the field, to running short of film because he didn't reload at the end of a game — and he's always checking these things as he moves to make his picture. "Every time now," he says, "I try to remember every mistake I've ever made and try to overcome it by checking all of those things."

Martin had positioned himself along the ropes at the Ryder Cup final hole. As the celebration started among Crenshaw and his teammates, Martin found himself in a shifting crowd along the rope. But he had a clear idea of where he wanted to be. Martin worked his way through the crowd and got to the spot he wanted by not giving up. "I think of angles," he says, "and I'm constantly planning."

Knowing what he wanted and having a plan in mind paid off. He got in a good spot and made up the rest of the distance by holding his camera out at arm's length between some celebrants and making the picture.

Martin's laws: be determined, be ready, have a plan. And, always make sure your shoes are tied securely.

If the action or reaction lags, follow Kennedy's example and look for the actions of a player to give you a picture. Got an infielder blowing bubbles? An outfielder doing stretching exercises during the game? A catcher with dirt all over him, or a group of bench warmers wearing their hats at odd angles? Any of these will make a picture when the action doesn't give you one.

The key to good coverage is to see a vari-

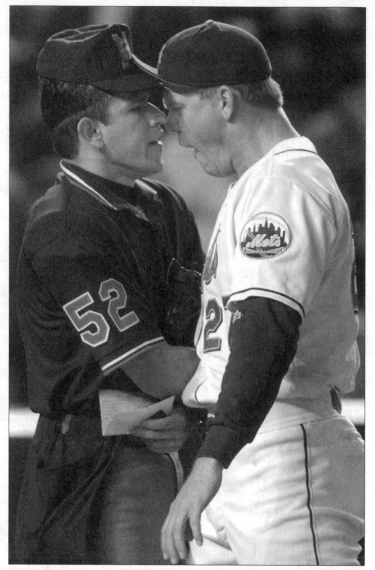

AP photographer Mark Lennihan stayed with a 1999 argument between umpire Alfonzo Marquez and New York Mets pitcher Dennis Cook and caught the moment when the two had a meeting of the minds, or at least their noses and the bills of their caps.

ety of pictures. Over the course of a season, follow Risberg's suggestion and try to shoot from several different perspectives, always looking for a different picture than you had from the game before.

Another way of expanding your sports

coverage is to look for subjects that will make interesting photo essays.

Susan Ragan saw stories in the sports pages about a young jockey, Julie Krone, who was quickly making a name for herself. Ragan contacted the jockey's agent and proposed a story. The result was an interesting look at a sport that generally doesn't get much coverage.

But it wasn't as easy as Ragan's pictures make it look. Ragan found that Krone, despite her fame, was very self-conscious. "Her father is a photographer and she's very conscious of the camera," Ragan says. "It took much longer

For an essay on jockey Julie Krone, right, AP photographer Susan Ragan spent several hours over a series of days with Krone, often not even making a picture.

with her to break through that shell. There were days when I had nothing, but I kept going back and finally she mellowed out."

Good pictures can happen at any level of sports.

Amy Sancetta's picture of a high school basketball player agonizing over a loss in the state tourney while the winners cele-

brate is a solid storyteller.

"I was going for a good picture of the girl on the ground, and the others danced through the frame," Sancetta says. "I was lucky."

But that luck resulted from some planning. Sancetta had followed the story of the game, as well as the action. She knew the player on the ground was not only the top scorer, but also had caused a turnover for her team late in the game. The other team had converted that turnover for the lead and the championship.

Sancetta knew "it was more important to get a good picture of the key player, than a good picture of just any player." That's why she went for the dejection, rather than move on to the jubilation. She moved into a position to make the picture and the jubilation rounded out the image.

Early training, to focus on the details,

paid off years later for Sancetta as she followed St. Louis Cardinals slugger Mark McGwire on his chase for the home run title.

Knowing they had a few games to get into a groove with McGwire, Sancetta and other AP photographers on the home run chase crew studied the Cards slugger to learn everything they could about how he handled the bat, how he reacted, what his habits were.

And Sancetta tried different shooting positions, too, to make sure she'd have the picture she wanted when the big home run finally came. Sancetta knew she would have to sit on a stool among the fans in the first row over the wall on the third base line, but she had some say on which aisle to use.

"I had my choice of several aisles," she says, "so well before the games, when I first got there, I sat in those spots trying to find where the third base coach would stand, where I might be blocked." Once she settled on her spot, she went through her lenses to see which would give her the framing she wanted.

"You have to know how McGwire swings the bat for your timing on contact," Sancetta explains, "as well as what he does after he hits it." Ken Griffey Jr., another slugger who had a hot year that season, "flips his bat down real fast, but McGwire likes to hold his bat up there and linger, linger, linger."

That knowledge would alert her to pictures that could be made as McGwire tied, then broke the record.

And when the big home runs happened, Sancetta wanted to make as much out of

the situation as possible. "I wanted to not just shoot it once," she says. "I wanted to be able to shoot them twice which meant shooting two cameras at the same time." Each camera gave her a slightly different view, one horizontal with the umpire, catcher and fans watching the ball, too. The other was vertical and much tighter.

With a remote camera next to her on a

Amy Sancetta's coverage of Mark McGwire breaking the home run record took planning. She had a plan to make the swing and reaction on at least two cameras (above), and then to follow McGwire as he rounded the bases (opposite).

tripod, which she fired with a foot switch, Sancetta hand held the other camera on a monopod.

She watched McGwire's batting habits so much she not only knew how he would react, but even had a pretty good idea when he was going to swing. "When McGwire would make a move like he was going to swing," she explains, "I would push the button on the camera in my hand and hit the foot switch."

Not every swing produced a home run and Sancetta sometimes ended up with nothing to show for her efforts. But, she'd reload and be ready the next time.

When the record-setting home run came on the final day of the season, Sancetta had McGwire on two cameras watching the flight of the ball from the plate. She also

AP photographer Mark Duncan was ready to drop his telephoto lens when Jacksonville Jaquars quarterback Mark Brunell hurdled some Cleveland Browns defenders at the goal line in a 1999 game.

shot him as he trotted around the bases and broke into a big grin. She had the scene lensed perfectly and caught McGwire celebrating with a fan's sign prominent in the background.

The idea of planning and preparation is a common thread.

Cabluck says, "You have to think ahead. In football, for instance, you need to have a feeling for the quarterback and know what he is thinking. If it's third down and eight

yards, you know it's going to be a pass play. That's just doing your homework, knowing how the game is played."

When Franco Harris of the Pittsburgh Steelers scored a touchdown on the legendary catch known as the "immaculate reception," Cabluck was waiting in the end zone to make the picture as Harris came toward him.

The other team had just scored, and the Steelers were a touchdown behind and starting their drive a considerable distance from their goal line. "You have to think what is going to happen that is going to be significant," Cabluck says. "The only thing that would happen to change the game would be a Steeler crossing the goal line to score."

You just can't plan and study too much.

Doug Mills watched U.S. sprinter Michael Johnson closely as he covered the U.S. squad's trials before the 1996 Olympics in Atlanta. Johnson was one of the favorites in the dashes and Mills knew he'd want a special picture of him at the Olympics.

During the trials, Mills noticed that Johnson reacted to his win by throwing his arms in the air a stride or two past the finish line. When the Olympics rolled around, Mills realized that the timing clock had been moved. It appeared that Johnson would be reacting to his win as he passed in front of the sign.

Mills thought, "Wow, if this guy would break the world record, it would be nice to

Doug Mills of the AP had seen Michael Johnson react to a win in the trials the month before so he was ready with five remote cameras, in addition to the ones he was using in his camera position, to capture Johnson after his world record effort in the 200 meters at the 1996 Olympic Games.

have those two elements," the clock and Johnson. One problem, though. Mills quickly realized that the best angle couldn't be seen from his photo position at the end of the straightaway.

"I couldn't make it from where I was by hand," he said. So, Mills set up five remote cameras at various spots to maximize his chances of making the key moment. Johnson won the 200 meters, set a world record, and his reaction was everything Mills could hope for.

Mills hoped one of the cameras would pay off. After he shipped the film, he took

his setups down and got into the darkroom about fifteen minutes after the race. His editor handed him four rolls of film and relayed the news that there was nothing usable on the take. Mills went back out to the empty track and sat there for several minutes, examining the film, trying to figure out what had happened. "I was devastated," he recalls.

"It didn't dawn on me that the fifth roll hadn't come out of the processor yet," Mills said. Thinking that his efforts were for nothing, he finally headed back into the darkroom to pack up for the trip to the

Coverage Tips

Baseball

• If no one is on base and the batter is right-handed, try focusing on the third baseman or shortstop. They are most likely to handle any ground balls. A left-handed batter probably will hit it toward the first or second baseman.

• If a runner is on second or third, be prepared to cover home plate since any hit, or a long fly ball, will move the runner.

• If a runner is on first, with one out, be prepared to swing to second base to get the double-play attempt. If the pitcher is at bat, watch for the bunt.

• Always make a few frames of the starting pitchers. They will figure in the game story, win or lose.

• If a slugger is at bat, drop your coverage of the rest of the game and concentrate on the batter. If he hits a homer, it's a good picture, and if he strikes out, it is significant and he may react to the lost chance.

• When a batter hits a home run, swing your coverage over to the pitcher to get reaction. Until the batter rounds second base, you can't see his face anyway. Move back to the batter as he passes third and gets congratulations from the third base coach and the players at home plate.

Football

• Cover the quarterback from behind the line of scrimmage to cut down on the number of players between you and your subject.

• Use long lenses and work from farther down field to reduce the angle and open up your coverage zone. Ground plays will come at you and you'll be in a better position to cover pass plays, too.

• On fourth down in a kicking situation, move behind the line of scrimmage to cover the blocked kick or kicker's jubilation.

• For a good jubilation picture, position yourself between the driving team's bench and their scrimmage line when they are in a scoring position. When a team scores, the players usually run back toward their bench celebrating.

• If it is a very cold day, go to the side of the field facing into the sun and try for a backlit picture of the players breathing. It is a nice feature.

Basketball

• Move toward the sides of the court and shoot back in toward the basket with an 85 mm-105 mm lens to isolate the action and neutralize the background.

• Using a 180 mm lens, work the midcourt area. The lighting will be better because you aren't shooting up into a black backdrop. And, the pictures can be better because you'll get more eye level contact and fewer armpits and elbows in your photos.

• Watch the coaches for reaction to give your sports editor something to use as a sidebar. The story will always have coaches' comments.

• If the gym is badly lit, try shooting from some elevation. By shooting with the lights, instead of into them, your negatives will have much better exposure. Also, rim action from straight on gives a different perspective.

Golf

• Study the course map and find combinations of holes you can cover easily to give you the most chances to catch the leaders in a variety of situations.

• For insurance, make a few frames of the top golfers teeing off early in the round.

• Don't line up exactly with the hole and golfer. Try for an off-line setup to avoid distracting the player.

• Watch your background. If possible, move to a position that provides a neutral backdrop, like a grove of trees. A bright sky as a background will make calculating your exposure much more difficult.

hotel. As he came down the hall, another AP photographer congratulated him on his picture. Confused, Mills went into the darkroom to discover that the fifth roll of film had a terrific picture on it and the calls of congratulations were already starting to come in from around the country.

"I had gone from the lowest moment in my career," Mills says, "to the highest. I was on cloud nine."

So all the planning and thought paid off.

AP photographer David Guttenfelder was alert to pictures even during the national anthems at a soccer match in Nigeria and the attention paid off as young Nigerian boy got to be part of the Mexican squad.

Meanwhile, Biever thinks he has an advantage because he loves sports.

"Being a sports fan helps a lot," he says. For instance, "knowing that a team is a passing team, I'll stay downfield."

Biever spends his spare time reading sports magazines and catching sports shows on television when he isn't at an event. He knows photographers who regularly shoot sports but claim not to have an interest, but he thinks it is valuable to have the kind of knowledge that can only come from paying close attention.

But, Biever doesn't have to read many magazines or watch much TV to get basic knowledge of football. He grew up around it. Biever's dad, Vernon, is an award-winning football photographer with more than

fifty years as the team photographer for the Green Bay Packers. In fact, both men have won Pro Football Hall of Fame top photo awards, the only father-son duo to earn that distinction.

The younger Biever got his start trailing his dad on the sidelines at Packer games and snared his first published photo, a pan picture ("I must have set the camera wrong because I don't think I knew what a pan was.") of Packers great Bart Starr in action. Biever was 14 when it ran as a doubletruck in Look magazine.

Being a fan, or having a solid knowledge of what you are covering. Either way, it is going to give you a better than average shot at bringing home a good picture.

Cabluck was a regular at baseball playoffs and World Series for several years. In the weeks leading up to the championship games, Cabluck would try to see as many televised games as possible.

Like an opposing team's scouts, Cabluck would chart the tendencies of the players so he could anticipate their actions when he covered them in post-season play.

Add Sancetta's vote to those who say you have to think like you're in the game, like you are the runner on first base.

"Anticipate what they are going to do, just like the runner is, the pitcher is and the catcher is."

Binks says you learn in a lot of different ways. He learned from other photographers and from sitting next to Ernie, the ballboy at Baltimore's Memorial Stadium, "telling you what is going on. When you know the sport," Binks says, "and especially when you have the chance to cover the same team for a long time, then you begin to use anticipation and reaction. When you can anticipate and react as fast as the player does, then you've got it. You're synching with them."

Reinke believes you're going to have a tough time of it if you expect to make good pictures just by showing up at the stadium. A knowledge of the game and the participants is critical, he says.

Risberg says he takes advantage of all the material available about the sport he is covering at the time. "I always try to read the basic newspaper stories, but more than that, I read the handouts in the press box, the game notes and the statistics."

There is a lot there to help the photographer, Risberg says. "Many times I've gone to the ballpark and read the press releases and found a half-dozen ideas of things to watch for. You get some great tips just by reading the press handout sheets that many people throw away."

"What I try to do," Risberg says, "is come up with a combination of doing my homework, and mix that with instinct and experience. Sports photography is something where experience really counts."

Risberg uses a picture of Greg LeMond

Suggestions

Courtney O'Neill: "Don't be afraid to fail. Take risks, take chances, go out there with all of your senses on." She says to get out there and work at being a storyteller. "Not just through your eyes, but really getting out there and getting to know people. Give of yourself to the people, to your subject."

Ami Vitale: Don't hesitate when given the chance to try something new. "The best thing is to not be afraid."

Laura Rauch: "You are going to have to make those mistakes. That is the only way you can really learn. Part of the journey is to learn from your mistakes, and it also makes you a better photographer."

J. Pat Carter: "Know when to listen."

Pat Sullivan: Keep reminding yourself "not to take things for granted or to go by rote."

in a San Francisco bike race as an example. All the other photographers were at the top of the steep hill, but Risberg knew

Photographers should also be looking around on the sidelines and on off days at practices for good pictures. Ed Reinke caught Steve Young warming up during a smoky 1995 Super Bowl halftime show (top), Morry Gash made a good feature on then-Green Bay Packers coach Mike Holmgren leaving practice on his motorcycle in 1998 (above), and Doug Pizac captured Utah Jazz star Greg Ostertag chatting on his cell phone during a 1999 team practice (right).

Away from the field of play

Eric Gay shot San Antonio NBA player Steve Kerr getting iced down after a 1999 workout (top, left), Eric Risberg paid a visit to the range to make a photo of Tiger Woods getting help in 2000 from coach Butch Harmon (top, right) and Paul San-cya went to the bullpen to photograph relief pitcher John Rocker during his brief stint in the minor leagues in 2000 (above).

from following biking that "if there was going to be any good expression it would be near the bottom where the rider tackles the hill. I positioned myself halfway, where the rider would shift gears. He had a problem, and I made a picture of him tumbling," Risberg says. "Knowing the sport and going where the other photographers aren't paid off. I've always tried to listen to my instincts. Sometimes it's better, but it's always different."

Says Reinke, "You have to be acutely aware of what is happening in the game and what is happening around you. And you have to read the sports pages to know the people. You have to know what to expect next. That is why I just can't fathom someone making a good basketball picture, for instance, without knowing something about basketball."

"The other part of the preparation," Sancetta says of her McGwire coverage, "was just being excited about it. This was a home run race, a national phenomenon that had everyone glued to the TV and everyone talking about it over their morning coffee. So part of the preparation," she says, "was feeling that excitement and being up for it."

Binks says he learned about covering football by watching former *Washington Post* photographer Dick Darcy work the sidelines at Redskins games. Darcy would move up and down, Binks says, using an old zoom lens that had other photographers scratching their heads. But when they picked up the paper the next day, Darcy had the pictures. "He knew his stadium, he knew his angles," he knew what to expect in any given situation, Binks says. Darcy taught Binks to learn about the stadium and what different angles would provide, then learn everything you could about the players so you could anticipate their actions.

Binks says, "If you're working at ballparks you know well, and you know your players, you've got half the battle won. The rest is up to your reaction and your knowl-

Eric Risberg of the AP used his knowledge of bicycle racing to pick a spot where he thought riders might have problems in a San Francisco race. Risberg's planning paid off with a good picture as cyclist Greg LeMond took a tumble right in front of him.

edge of the game and your technical expertise."

And, Binks says, "He taught me to shoot football down on my knee because that is how the players see it." Biever agrees with that perspective. He also shoots from a kneeling position because he feels it brings more impact to his pictures.

Thinking about the way the game is played. Thinking about the people who play the games. Thinking about where the game is played. That knowledge will help your coverage.

Sancetta got a good picture at a tennis match because she knew the personalities of the participants. She was in a position to make a picture of tennis player John McEnroe kicking an intruding television camera because she knew that with McEnroe, "the good, different pictures are going to happen off the court because he is so volatile." When other photographers dropped their lenses during a break, Sancetta stayed on the temperamental star.

She agrees that studying what you cover is important. "I think what makes some people better at sports is they know the sports they cover."

Ragan, to make up for a lack of sports

Instead of setting her cameras down during a change of sides at a Philadelphia tennis match, AP photographer Amy Sancetta stayed alert because mercurial player John McEnroe was on the court. Sure enough, McEnroe made a statement on his feelings about television coverage by pushing a camera away with his foot. Sancetta had the picture.

interest and training as a child, prepares for her assignments by doing as much research as possible. "I read a bunch of stuff because I wasn't raised to know it," she says.

Ragan is usually nervous as she nears game time, and tries to distance herself from the noise and clamor of the sports scene. "Mentally I try not to think of it too much because I worry too much. But as soon as the event starts, it goes away. My adrenaline kicks in and I start thinking through my eyes or something. There can be billions of people around, but I am into myself. When people talk, I don't hear them."

Photographer Robert Bukaty of the AP watched the action at the snowboarding venue at the 1998 Olympics in Japan, then took a spot where he thought he could make the best action. It paid off with this great moment of a Norwegian competitor during a training run for the halfpipe competition.

She says she becomes very focused. "My mind never wanders. I anticipate things without thinking about it. It's instinct, I think."

While motor-driven cameras give photog-raphers the benefit of having lots of frames to pick from, Cabluck believes the best discipline comes from following the practices of the photographers in the Speed Graphic days.

That discipline, Cabluck says, caused you "to anticipate peak of action in sports, because in those days it was 4x5, one shot, and the shutters wouldn't always freeze the action. So you had to have the peak of action, because at the peak there is less motion."

"It's easier now to go out and machine gun from the hip," and have several frames to select from, but it takes "less discipline," says Cabluck, who concedes that he often uses a motor drive.

Several top sports photographers say they try to make the first exposure of a sequence, the key frames, then they let the motor run off a few more frames for fol-lowup protection. These photographers say they have found that hitting the motor early often leaves them with the key pic-ture "between" frames.

Biever thinks it is better to think single frame. "I am looking for a picture before I shoot it," he says.

And, when it comes to equipment, Ris-berg says that sometimes less is better. "One of the things that has worked well for me has been to travel light." He refrains from "taking three or four cameras with every focal-length lens I have to a game." Instead, he works "primarily with two cam-eras -- one with a long lens, one with an intermediate zoom."

Binks says he finds working with the zooms is a big help because it cuts down on the amount of equipment he has to handle. "The advent of the fast zoom has brought the sports photographer up to speed with having a variety of lenses in one." With the zoom, Binks says, he can cover "pregame headshots, a feature in the stands, or a play at home plate."

"I use a zoom preset" at a focal length, Binks says. "I use it as though I had all of those lenses in my bag. When I get to messing with zooming it in and out, I'm dead." And, that's part of knowing your equipment and how it works best for you.

That simplistic approach pays off when you have to react quickly, Risberg says. "Too many times, I see people making it very difficult for themselves by trying to take everything. Keeping it simple has allowed me to have great mobility in situations where you have to move quickly to capture a breaking moment."

Reinke warns not to travel too light, though.

"You go to a basketball game," Reinke says, "and you are thinking a 300 and an 80-200 zoom. You're thinking you want to shoot this end of the court and the other end of the court. I see people come to a basketball game and they only have those two lenses on two cameras." Reinke thinks they are going to be scrambling if the unexpected happens.

Mike Conroy of the AP knew Mateen Cleaves of Michigan State was the most valuable player in the final game of the 2000 NCAA Final Four championship in Indianapolis so he stayed with him through the celebration and postgame television interviews on the court. Sticking with his plan paid off for Conroy when Cleaves reacted as he left the court and was greeted by his mother and proud father.

Minutes before a postseason basketball game, the nation's top player that year passed in front of Reinke on crutches and sat down on the team's bench with his coach.

"I reached into my bag, pulled out the wide angle lens, set it right down on the floor beside him," Reinke explains. "It is one of the few moments you can get that kind of access, that kind of intimacy.

Getting in the door

Access is the name of the game in coverage of news, sports and feature stories. Being close to what is going on, or in a good vantage spot, is more times than not going to pay off in better pictures.

But the importance of that access is heightened in the world of sports, it seems, because more events at all levels are being closely managed with controls brought on by broadcast rights, increased crowd control and athletes' privacy and security concerns.

That doesn't mean photographers have to miss out on a good position, though.

According to Gary Kemper, who has served as the photo chief for the 1996 Atlanta and 2000 Sydney Olympic Games after a career with several news agencies, there is a way for photographers to work for more access and have their ideas and suggestions heard by organizers.

The secret, he says, is to do your homework and get there early.

That's good advice for covering sports but will also work for any kind of organized event from the county council meeting to a national political convention.

"The biggest element in all this is getting in early," he says. "Getting in early, getting to know the people who are involved in the event and assuring them that they can have a level of com-

Working in advance with the organizers of the 1994 Olympics in Lillehammer got access for AP photographer Diether Endlicher to make this view of the Olympic torch being brought into opening ceremonies by a ski jumper.

fort that whatever you are doing will not have an impact on the event."

From the organizer's standpoint, Kemper says, "The fear is a disruption. You need to assure them that nothing that you are doing is going to interfere but rather to enhance their event. Then, I think, you are going to be a lot more successful."

That is true even while covering high school sports, Kemper says.

Photographers will earn more access by putting in some time before the big game, not getting there as the whistle blows and expecting to go where they want. "Photographers should go to practices, get to know the coach, the players and, if possible, the officials," Kemper says. "Consistently show up and do things throughout the season and by the end of the season you can do a lot of things that they (the organizers) would have not trusted earlier."

That trust will result in access to better shooting positions. "Once they get to know you and know your professionalism, doors will open," he says. "You'll make better technical pictures, and better pictures of people. You might get into places -- the dressing room, for instance -- that you might not have before."

Better pictures from some different spots — a good payback for an early investment of time.

That's the kind of prepared you want to be," according to Reinke who watched as other photographers scrambled to make the picture from father back with their longer glass.

And, once you've got the picture, don't forget to give the editor enough caption information to work with.

"In at least the first general edit of a deadline shoot," Binks says, "I rely on what the photographer has given me on the caption bag."

At a football game, Binks says, they might not realize it "but the photographer does the first edit by giving me a star on a key play, or a key interception, and gives me the down and the time and the quarter. That's one of the great failings of sports photographers in particular, and most photographers in general. They don't provide the kind of caption information that makes the editor's job easier."

Binks says "A good editor will find the good picture on the film, but then you have to tell the layout person what the picture means, why you picked it." You may tell the layout person it's a good picture, but that team may have lost.

Dan Hulshizer of the AP wasn't sure what he had until he got a look at the images after shooting goalie Brian Boucher of the Philadelphia Flyers making a rather unorthodox stop on a shot in a 2000 Stanley Cup playoffs match -- the puck stuck in Boucher's mask.

The layout person is generally looking for the most significant picture. Binks says "there is a real misunderstanding about that." The photographer should be asking, "Do I have the moment here? I find it is much easier to push the ones that tell the game story; they stand on their own."

But, the editor has to know it's the right selection. Binks says of shooting sports: "You've got to be a reporter. When you are a reporter and a photographer, you capture the key moments and you mark those on the bags."

Lessons

Horst Faas: "Concentrate on a few good moments"

J. Pat Carter: "You've got to keep gathering knowledge"

Alan Diaz: "The minute it opened, I shot 'em"

David Guttenfelder: The people are really the story

David Longstreath: You're in the business to make pictures, not excuses

Charles Rex Arbogast: Doing your homework pays off

David Guttenfelder: Working in a human storm

David Martin: "You have to get wet to get the best pictures"

David Phillip, Pat Sullivan: "It can get repetitive shooting flowers..."

Remotes: A second way to see

Horst Faas
"Concentrate on a few good moments"

The career of Horst Faas, a senior photo editor in the AP's London bureau, has taken him to the Congo, to Vietnam, to Dacca, and many other stops along the road.

And each place, each experience along that road, was filed away to be used another time when faced with a tough or perplexing situation.

But the very basis for his actions years later, which got him safely in and out of the world's hot spots, were forged in his youth.

Coming of age in Germany during and after World War II, Faas learned important lessons. One was how to be careful. "I was trained all through my youth to watch my step," Faas says. "Growing up in six years of war and the time after the war, you had to watch everything. Physically, it was important to do the right thing. This way of life formed a discipline."

Those lessons paid off years later when he was working among hostile crowds in the Congo or a mob taking out vengeance on enemies in Dacca.

Faas' education in photography also proved to be an exercise in discipline.

He grew up without photography for the most part, except for the pictures in the

weekly newsmagazines, which he found exciting. But his dream was to be a writer. That led to him reading Hemingway, Faulkner and Greene.

When it was time for Faas to find work, he was hired to help restore a Munich agency's photo library, which had been ransacked in the closing days of the war. Studying those prints as he filed them away gave him an appreciation for content and composition and, just as important, what would sell.

But the content was what caught his eye. "I got excited by what you can do with photography," Faas says.

From the library, he progressed to a job in the agency's darkroom mixing chemicals. Then, drying prints. Then, after a time, he began processing film.

Next on the agenda was making prints. The printmaking carried a lesson. You had to learn to work quickly, but just as important, you had to learn to make prints without wasting paper. "You were quickly out of it again, if you make mistakes and waste paper," Faas recalls.

That's how it worked in those days. You progressed as you learned the stages of your craft. More of that discipline.

Finally, Faas was issued a camera and sent out to make pictures. That came with an added responsibility. You not only had to make pictures, but you were expected to sell them to local newspapers and magazines, too.

Another learning experience.

"Taking pictures is one thing," Faas says. "Selling is another. Everyone was a critic. You had to produce something that they liked and bought and appreciated."

Faas thinks this progression -- library, darkroom, photography, sales, editing -- gave him a better understanding of not only what was a good photo, but also a good grounding in the whole process.

"The editing began with the camera," Faas says. There were only twelve frames on a roll and someone back at the office was keeping an eye on how much film he shot, so he learned to shoot only when he was sure he had something.

"Unless you could see the picture being published," Faas said, "and you knew that by looking at fifteen papers each day, you didn't take the picture." No motor drive sequences for those photographers. "You tried to concentrate on a few good moments."

That was a lesson Faas has carried throughout his career. Except in rare cases, he prefers to use single-shot cameras.

Faas' first international assignment of note with the AP was an uprising in the Congo. Again, lessons were learned. "I cultivated local sources and tried to make local friends," he says. And he learned some of the local language. "That always paid off."

Taking pictures in the Congo often was a test of courage. "Picture-taking was easy if you had the guts to raise your camera when they said no. But getting the feel for it and getting there," he says, "was only possible through good local contacts."

Lessons learned decades ago that carry through to today.

Pictures like this one of young members of a Katanga youth group in 1961 were easy to make if you cultivated good local contacts, according to Horst Faas.

"What applies still today," Faas says, "is you should not be noticed by extraordinary behavior or clothing or language."

Faas is convinced that the access news people had in Vietnam, his next war, was earned. It was earned, he says, "by walking three miles with the troops. That earned respect and because of that respect, we were welcomed back by certain units and they helped us get places."

And, Faas believes, the unwritten code of conduct journalists followed there also earned them the respect that helped them to do their job.

"First of all," Faas says, "when you are privileged to be in a place where extraordi-

A father holds his child's body as South Vietnamese soldiers look on from an armored personnel carrier after the child was killed during fighting in a village near the Cambodian border in 1964. The photograph was part of war coverage that won Horst Faas of the AP his first Pulitzer Prize.

pictures made by Faas and others were accepted "as the ugly reality of Vietnam."

His coverage of the war won him the 1965 Pulitzer Prize for news photography.

Looking back at his years in Vietnam, Faas doesn't feel nostalgia. What he remembers are the colleagues who were killed or wounded trying to bring the story to the world.

nary things are happening, you do not poke your lens into someone's face who is dying. You either feel, or you don't feel. This is not a rule you can write down. Someone who breaks these rules is not a sensitive person, not a good photographer. You have to have a feeling for these borderline situations. In a war situation, this is obvious."

Faas, who was wounded by shrapnel while covering a battle, saw the war for what it was, brutal and nasty. "When something is brutal and nasty, then you should try to show it as harsh and nasty as it is." In Vietnam, Faas says, "torture was an everyday thing. If you want to do something about it, you should show it." The

"When I left," Faas says, "I tried to leave it behind me. It wasn't my country or my war. I was just privileged to be there to report." Pressed as to how he felt about his years covering the war, Faas replies simply, "I still don't look back with nostalgia. I can't forget the nasty things and just remember the good things."

From Vietnam, Faas covered events in other parts of the world, eventually landing in Dacca, Bangladesh, in the middle of an uprising that left hundreds dead or mutilated.

Just as he had in Vietnam, Faas felt an obligation to show the world what was happening, but the reality of it sickened him.

Rival factions had been fighting and eventually one side prevailed. To show its power, the winning faction held a rally in a soccer stadium and brought in captured foes.

What happened next, a frenzy of violence and torture, was as horrifying as anything Faas had seen in his years in Vietnam and Africa.

"Emotionally, it was awful," Faas says of the scene "and to live through it even as a spectator was awful." Some journalists had avoided the scene, others left as the violence escalated. Faas and AP colleague Michel Laurent stayed.

"It wouldn't have been right to walk away from it," Faas says. "I would say there is a certain obligation to see it through and to present a report that says this is what happened."

There were times when Faas and Laurent wondered if they should slip away, but they felt the need to keep making pictures.

"I had to see it through," Faas says. "I couldn't disappear in the middle of it. We were trapped there, fascinated, trapped watching it."

When the violence ebbed, Faas and Laurent slipped away. Faas used his Indian army accreditation to secure travel to Calcutta, where he filed the first pictures early the next morning. Others, rejected by censors, were shipped by courier to London, where they were transmitted the next day.

Laurent and Faas were awarded the 1972 Pulitzer Prize for news photography for their coverage. The award made Faas the first photographer in the prize's history to win two.

Members of the winning faction bayonet captives from the losing side during a rally in a Dacca soccer stadium after a civil war in Bangladesh in 1971.

Through all of these experiences, Faas knew he was there to report and make pictures.

"These things happen without you being able to do anything about it," Faas says. "This isn't a spectacle where you can just bug out."

His advice to the photojournalists of today, based on the lessons he has learned, is straight to the point. "You aren't there to lecture and pontificate. The only thing that you should be concerned about is to present photographs that tell the story so people can understand what is happening."

J. Pat Carter
"You've got to keep gathering knowledge"

When a tornado's funnel cloud begins to fill your frame, and you are using a wide angle lens, you know you're close.

And that is not to say that Oklahoma City AP photographer J. Pat Carter is reckless about his approach to covering the storms that sweep through his area every spring and fall.

"I don't go into these things half-cocked," he says. "I have some basic knowledge that I have gained." One of those basics is to use a scanner in his truck to keep up with reports from weather spotters, the local media and emergency services personnel.

Carter also has a high-tech tool he uses. "In my laptop, I even have a program

where I can download instant weather images using my cell phone," he says. "I try to learn as much as I can before going to it."

Another tool is much more basic -- a good local road map. By studying the map as he approaches the storm, Carter can find possible escape routes.

Carter had been covering the deadly storms since 1972 but had never gotten a picture of a funnel cloud on the ground. As he set out one day in May 1999, that was

After riding out the high winds and blowing debris as a tornado passed over them, AP photographer J. Pat Carter made this photo of the twin funnel clouds moving away from him and the family who had taken refuge with him under a bridge overpass outside Newcastle, Okla., in 1999.

about to change. "My goal that night was to get a funnel on the ground," he says. But, he buffered that drive with a healthy respect for the quick changing conditions. "I'd be crazy to say I wasn't afraid. If you lose that respect or that fear, you are a fool."

As he listened to reports about the storm's enormous size and destructive power, Carter made his move to come in from one side of it. "This funnel was on the ground for sixteen miles," he says, "and they had been talking and talking about it. I wanted to come in from the side so I wouldn't be caught in the path of it."

But because of the intensity of the rain, hail and lightning, Carter opted for a more direct approach.

"I decided the only way to get it was to drive to it," he says. Some might question the wisdom of that approach, but Carter believed he had the situation under control.

"You could see the storm coming. I could see the clouds. I could see where it was."

Driving along a nearly deserted interstate highway, Carter spotted a funnel cloud and began to make pictures. First, using a 400 mm lenses with a 2x tele-extender, then switching to a 1.4x extender, then a 300, then an 80-200 zoom. Carter decided at that point to stick it out and let the storm catch up to him.

He moved his truck three times as he made pictures and looked for shelter. Keeping an eye on his road map, he kept an escape route in the back of his mind.

He considered pulling off under one overpass, but "a little voice told me not to stop there." That turned out to be a good call as he later learned one person was killed and several other were injured at that spot. "Something just wasn't right about it," he says. "I used my experience, my knowledge, my gut feelings like in baseball when you have a runner on first base, but you think you should pay attention to the batter. It was just something that comes with experience."

At the next underpass, Carter was going to ride out the storm because it was starting to catch up with him. "It all started happening. The funnel was roughly three football fields away," he remembers.

As he pulled under the span, he saw a woman struggling to get her two kids out of her van. "I yelled to her to take cover," he says, but the wind was blowing so hard she couldn't get the door open. It took Carter's help to finally get the youngsters from the van.

"The wind was so strong and stuff was hitting us like you wouldn't believe." he says. "I'm yelling at her to take cover and trying to herd the kids to shelter. By the time I got the kids out of the truck, the funnel was two football fields away.

"I pushed her down with one child," he remembers, "and I had one of the children in my arms. I turned my back into the wind and got ready for the ride."

But Carter wasn't going to let the opportunity for an incredible photo pass him by. "The photographer did come out in me at this point. I thought, 'God, in case this is my last image,' and I stuck my arm out and I tried to make some frames."

But the wind was blowing so hard, he says, "I ended up with the perfect pan shot."

At this point, the storm was on top of them and Carter remembers it bringing torrents of debris -- car parts, fence posts, garbage, mud -- under the bridge. Carter says he is not a religious person, but he did say some prayers at that point. "I felt religion that day," he says.

The storm now was surrounding Carter and the family. "I looked up and the stuff was going north to south on one side of us and south to north on the other side. We were in the middle of it." Carter remembers telling the little girl in his arms that they would survive. "This is as bad as it is going to get," he remembers telling her. "We are going to make it."

"Things were happening so fast under the bridge," he says. "I don't know if I was afraid or not. It may have been two minutes or so, but it seemed like a lifetime."

As the tornado passed over them and

began to move away, Carter says he "jumped up and I put my camera to my eye." But, the camera was covered with mud, "so I've got to clean off the rear eyepiece. Then I had to wipe off the front glass."

Carter quickly made sure the woman and her children were OK and that they knew where to go to stay out of the storm's path. Then he got himself together. And got ready to go back to work. The woman later told Carter that at this point he turned to her and said, "I've got to go make pictures!"

But, Carter's frightening experience wasn't over. The storm had changed direction and was headed for the suburb where he lives.

"I called my wife and yelled for her to take cover," he remembers. "This is when true panic sets in." As Carter trailed the storm, watching it destroy everything in its path, his cell phone went down.

But he continued to follow the storm. "This is the hardest decision I've had to make as a professional," he says. "Death and destruction on one hand, and, on the other hand, a wife at home."

"I chose death and destruction, but that's not as callous as it sounds. I could see rooftops in my neighborhood and I thought, 'If she has a rooftop, she's OK.'"

Carter followed the storm to a nearby neighborhood and began making pictures.

> "This is the hardest decision I've had to make as a professional. Death and destruction on one hand, and, on the other hand, a wife at home."
>
> —J. Pat Carter

He was fighting equipment problems because of the beating his cameras and lenses had taken under the bridge.

"It was an intense time," he says. "I shot pictures for maybe thirty minutes or an hour."

He then headed for his neighborhood, where he found his wife and his home both OK. There was no power or phones in the area, so Carter left for his office to file his pictures.

He knew what he had shot, but he wasn't sure how the pictures would turn out. Carter had shot the funnel cloud pictures using autoexposure and autofocus. "I was battling the wind and shooting a 15th or a 30th (of a second). I was afraid they (the family) would be too dark and the storm would be exposed right or they would be OK and the storm would be blown out."

Carter plugged his digital camera disk into his computer at the office and called up the pictures on the screen.

"I pulled my disk up on the screen," he says, "and said to myself 'Here's a funnel. Here's a funnel. I got this!'"

Carter transmitted the picture of the view from under the bridge and began preparing other pictures. About that time, one of his colleagues in the bureau pointed out that his picture had not one, but two funnels. "I never saw the one," he says. "I was watching the monster."

Meanwhile, that monster storm had

swept across the area damaging and destroying houses and businesses, as well as a school and a hospital. As he finished moving his pictures, Carter worked with local newspapers and freelance photographers who were covering the storm.

"Usually when you do a storm," he says, "you move your pictures and you go back out." But the endless stream of reports of death and destruction rocked Carter. "I sat there and that's when it hit me," he says. "I just didn't know where to go. It was just so big.

"It was the most helpless feeling I had ever had."

Knowing he had good pictures and being well aware of the danger of being out in the dark with wires down and debris in the streets, Carter went home to shower in the dark and change clothes.

Then, it was back out to do followup coverage. When reinforcements from other AP bureaus were delayed by lingering storms in the area, Carter worked with his local crew of freelancers.

That work went on for three days almost around the clock.

Carter finally had his funnel picture. But he also had even more respect for the power of nature and for the lessons that can be learned from covering something like the tornadoes he had just gone through.

"Each time you go out, you've got to weigh what's happening," he says. "There are no rules, no textbooks on how to cover this stuff. You've got to keep gathering knowledge and hope you are making the right decisions out there."

Alan Diaz
"The minute it opened, I shot 'em"

Elian.

The name of a 6-year-old boy from Cuba has become a name for a range of feelings.

Like Waco. Like Ruby Ridge. To some, a symbol of a heavy-handed U.S. government action. The symbol of freedom from the Castro regime. The youngster whose mother died trying to escape with him to a better life in America.

To others, Elian is the child caught in politics between two countries and between pro- and anti-Castro factions. The child kept from his father, then later reunited while the courts wrestled with his ultimate fate.

One picture has become the icon for that turmoil.

The picture, by Miami freelance photographer Alan Diaz, shows a heavily armed U.S. government agent reaching for Elian Gonzalez in the Miami home of his great-uncle where he was living.

That photo, shot on assignment for the Associated Press, captured the attention of the world in a way that few pictures ever do. It is the kind of photo that very well could be an enduring and powerful image for years and years to come.

Behind that picture is the story of Diaz, a

Five months of waiting turned into less than eight seconds of action for photographer Alan Diaz when government agents raided a Miami home in 2000 to regain custody of 6-year-old Elian Gonzalez. The youngster, who had been living with his relatives after he was rescued during an escape from Cuba, was taken to be reunited with his father. Diaz, the lone journalist to make it inside the house, had spent the five months of Elian's life in the Miami neighborhood examining different scenarios of how it might end. When it did happen, Diaz's primary plan worked to form and he had the pictures. On the following pages are the raw camera files from Diaz's digital camera with the time stamp of when the pictures were made.

52-year-old photographer raised in Cuba, just trying to do his job. Through the five months that the story centered on a simple home in a Miami neighborhood, Diaz spent countless hours there, more time there than any other journalist, making photographs of young Elian and the other members of the cast of the drama that was being played out.

And, all the while, Diaz was thinking about what might happen. How the drama might play out.

When it finally did, early on the Saturday morning of the Easter weekend, Diaz was the only journalist to get into the house and witness the action.

Other journalists tried but failed. But, Diaz, through his planning and quick action, was successful, a testimony to the countless details he had attended to during that long stakeout.

Photographers always wonder if they'll respond when the bell rings. Diaz did.

Ten days after that fateful Saturday morning, Diaz was interviewed.

This is his story.

How do you work in that kind of situation?

It is a long process. It was a long time. It was not like a usual story, like spot news or a story that runs for a week. I had months to go on this. I did develop a relationship with the family because you are sitting out there every day for months. The person in that house is either going to love you or they are going to hate you or he is going to call the cops on you.

Was it difficult to become part of that neighborhood scene?

I was lucky enough to speak Spanish, and understand the culture, understand what they were going through. Right or wrong wasn't my problem. I understood what they were going through.

We developed a relationship. More like a normal relationship like you would develop with your next-door neighbor. Honestly, I know more people on that block than I know on mine. I've made friends in that neighborhood, the kind of friends you have for a lifetime.

Neighbors that trusted me, left their van open so I could get in out of the sun, left me their house keys when they would go to work so I could go to the bathroom, transmit.

I had three houses, two on the block and one a block away because I had to secure places where I could transmit. I had three houses where they would leave me the keys if they'd go out so I could transmit.

I still don't believe it. In today's world for someone to leave you their keys to their house? No. 1, I have a ponytail. This long-haired guy. Cubans hate that. And, No. 2, you are the media. Cubans are very, very leery of the media.

For five months, shooting what I could. Shooting Elian going to school, coming out of the house.

> "I knew it was going to go down like this. I had it in my mind. I played it a million times. I played it out in my mind exactly as I executed it."

Did you think It would come down like it did? Did you have a game plan?

I knew it was going to go down like this. I had it in my mind. I played it a million times. I played it out in my mind exactly as I executed it. I knew I would have to jump the fence. For that, I made an arrangement with the owner of the next-door parking lot. Just next to the fence. All I had to do was jump the fence to get in. He gave me a prime spot there.

I knew this was going to go this way because of the pride in Lazaro [Lazaro Gonzalez, Elian's great-uncle]. He is a humble Cuban. They are very humble. They are not educated. They are just humble people but with a pride so big. I knew from the way he would express himself at times that this man would not just hand over the boy. Just knowing the government and all this, I said it is going to come down to this disaster. Many a time he would say, 'If it

Frame: DSC001 Time: 5:20:00

Frame: DSC002 Time: 5:20:50

happens, will you come in? Please come in.'

Not only to me, but also to TV. I would not have survived this without TV. There was a 24-hour crew there, doing shifts of 12 and 12. I developed a relationship with them. Everything I knew, I would tell them. Everything they knew, they would tell me.

I was alone. I was at a big disadvantage. I would work my 12-15 hours and then have to go home and sleep. It was only me and TV. The crew that would do the night and morning would call me if anything arose, like if they saw strange movements or something like that.

It took a lot of work and friendship. I ate, drank water, thanks to these guys. I would spend long hauls out there without coming home.

When did things really begin to happen?

Its starts on a Wednesday. I have a hunch something is going down. You could see it going on with the negotiations and the way the family was acting. Lazaro had a lot of stress on him. He was like a mad bull in

there. I knew he was negotiating and things weren't working out. Which was giving me the idea, 'Hey, this is going to go down,' because if it doesn't work out, they are going to come in.

I decide not to go home. The neighbor says if you want to, sleep in the house or in the van. But I wouldn't go in [the house] because to go in would be like going home. Minute I take a bed, I'll miss the whole world. So I took the van, but I couldn't sleep, because it was very noisy out there.

Then Thursday goes by. It's the same thing. I stay, and it didn't go down.

Then Friday, it was Good Friday. I said, 'Today's Good Friday, we shouldn't be working,' but I did my little prayer out there in the morning early and I just asked him for courage and strength because I really needed it because I was tired. I asked God, 'God, give me some strength to do this, because I am tired.'

In the afternoon, I get the idea, 'Man, this is going to go down.' My lenses are dirty. I've got to change my batteries.

So, I did all that, taking it easy there on

Frame: DSC003 Time: 5:20:52

Frame: DSC004 Time: 5:20:52

the side, sitting down. I changed the batteries on my strobe, put a new battery in the D-1, cleaned the lenses. I set the Quantum out with the cable and all so I could hook it up if I needed it.

About 1 in the morning, Lazaro comes out and gets to the fence. I can tell this man is under tremendous pressure. He says, 'Man, if it happens, please come in.'

All of a sudden at 5 o'clock in the morning, I'm standing and looking at the crowd, and I hear this noise in the back. I call it a stampede, but it's noise, it's a convulsion, it's a lot of strange noises in the back of Lazaro's home, which weren't normal. It was totally different than every day I had been there. I just ran to my bag, which is next to my seat, grabbed my D-1. I turned on the strobe, turned on the D-1, set the shutter at 125 because I knew there was going to be movement. And I just jumped the fence. As I jump the fence, I see the NBC guy jumping, but he falls down, camera and all. He's down on the floor. I just kept going. I run in the front door, which is open, and family members are shouting,

'They're here. They're here!'

All that stuff we saw on TV, that you see the guys come up in front of the house, the vans, I didn't see any of that. I beat them. I knew they were there because of all the noise that was going on back there.

So I got in. I land in the living room, which is very dark, and everybody is in there. They are very disoriented. A little crazy in there.

I say, 'Where is the kid,' and one of the family members points to the room and pushes me there. I knew which room was Elian's because it was the first room in the house. You could see him from outside and also I had been in there to shoot him twice before. I go to the room and it is pitch black in there. I couldn't see a thing. I saw the bed with something that resembled a kid sleeping. I said, 'I need light,' and I was lucky enough to just stretch my arm and was able to turn on the switch. I hit it on the first try. When it goes on, I realize there is no one in the room.

I get out and right in front of Marisleysis' [Marisleysis Gonzalez, Elian's cousin] room

Frame: DSC005 Time: 5:20:54

Frame: DSC006 Time: 5:20:54

is Lazaro's room and the door is closed. I start banging on the door, because he might be in there. Bang, bang, bang. Angela, Lazaro's wife, opens the door. She just looks at me. She never said a word to me. She just looks very dazed.

I walk in and see Donato [Donato Dalrymple, one of two fishermen who pulled Elian from the ocean] with Elian in his arms right there standing in the closet. The door is open in the closet and I looked at them. They looked straight at me.

I take a shot because I knew in my mind that they were going to bust my camera in my face. This is my thought. That was at the best because I always thought that it could be a bullet first. Honestly. I thought when they open that door and see that strobe hit 'em, they might think it is anything and they might shoot me or something.

I said, 'Let me take this shot first.' I grabbed the shot and I have Elian in the closet with Donato.

Donato says something to me and I answer back to him. The kid says some-

thing to me, and I tried to comfort him the best I could. I just looked at the door and waited for them.

They kicked the door down. The minute it opened, I shot 'em. And I just kept on shooting. That's it. I shot and shot and shot. That's it.

They told me to back off two times coming in and one time going out, because I did try to follow them. They never touched me. Never. He looked me straight in the eyes and I felt the look. I thought right there that that was it. The rifle is coming right at my face, but, no, he didn't do it. I just tried to do what I could do.

By then, it must have sounded like a war going on in the living room...

It was a war before they came in. I could hear shouting. I can't make out the words. It was like an earthquake in the house. The house would tremble. Outside, there was a lot of screaming and a lot of stuff going on. You can hear all this. But I was in the room, and I just had to wait for them to come in.

Frame: DSC007 Time: 5:20:58

Frame: DSC014 Time: 5:21:38

Did you have any second thoughts about how it worked out?

No, not this time. I think it is the first time in my life I didn't second-guess myself. Everything but the room I had played it in my mind. It was in a different room. That caught me by surprise, but I think I reacted well to it. I knew what I was doing.

What were your plans?

I had three plans — A, B and C. Why? Because I was in a prime spot. I always thought the feds would come in, before it goes down and would clear us from the spot knowing how good the spot was.

Much before this became a gang bang with ten thousand cameras out there, when it was nice and clear, I set up three ladders. One ladder was at the garage where I can get the kid in the back of the home because I knew where he played.

I set up a second ladder straight on to the main entrance, that door, and I knew that was a main spot because you've got people coming in and out of the house.

I would run from the garage door to the main door ladder to get the shots there, because that way I always had my spots secured. Nobody touched my ladders. It could have been because of the time I spent out there, but nobody questioned my spots.

Everyone was working at a disadvantage to me because I had my spots set up long before they arrived. The minute the barriers went up, I knew the cameras would come, and they would take up places. The last time the barriers went up, four or five weeks ago, I set up my three ladders.

I was alone here so I had to secure a spot. I couldn't afford to shoot the garage and have Lazaro walk out with somebody important in front and not get that shot. So I would shoot my things from the side and run to the main, and I was dead on that door, the main entrance.

Plus the arrangement I had made with the owner of the house next door, which I said I would only use in an emergency when I think this is going to go down.

How were you able to keep track of what was happening?

I'm right there. I'm listening to everything that was going on in that house. I could hear the phone ring. I heard the phone ring around 4 in the morning. I said, 'These negotiations are still going on.' Who is going to call a home at 4 with ten thousand lawyers inside. I was aware of everything going on inside. Someone would come out and I would ask them, 'How's things going?' And they would say, 'Lazaro is talking on the phone now.' So I was really aware of everything going on.

> "I did seven frames inside the room. I did seven more outside the room in the living room, this whole craziness going on."

You mentioned that you had three plans, in addition to pre-positioning the ladders at various spots. What were those plans and how did they work into how it finally played out?

'A' was the one that I had right there, that I played.

'B' was they took me out. I would go to the front entrance where the kid would be taken out and have the shot that ran on the cover of Newsweek with the kid in the arms of the lady agent. That photo. I ran that through my mind a million times, too.

'C' was if they kill the media, a federal action where they would clean the street. I would go to the next-door house, which is a doctor who lives there who had offered me his home. There was a side entrance to Lazaro's house and from there I play plan 'A.'

Were you able to make many pictures?

I did seven frames inside the room. I did seven more outside the room in the living room, this whole craziness going on. I go towards the back, because I knew there was no reason for me to go to the front because it was all over, because those guys were fast. So I go towards the back of the house. Then I get hit with pepper spray, which was seeping in from the outside. It hit me right in the face.

There was a mask, but I never took it on. I had said to myself, 'I can't shoot with a mask. I'd rather suffer all this and work it out.'

I go out the back, and I get hit by the pepper spray in the face. Oh, God, I'm burning, I'm burning, I'm burning.

As I walk around the side of the house, I see all this going on and I lift my camera. As I lift my camera, my eyes are burning. I said, 'Wait a minute. I'm done.' I don't feel like shooting anymore. I'm tired. I think everything just hit me. I felt the weight of everything on me. So I went to the front of the house and I sat on the steps behind some bushes, so I couldn't be seen. I don't know why I did that. I wanted to be alone.

Sitting there, I hear Pete [AP photographer Pete Cosgrove] say, "Al, Al!" I hear my name and I just peek. I'm just trying to get this whole load off my body. I pull out my disk and hand it to him and go back to my spot behind the bushes and called in to let them know it had gone down.

It looks like your planning paid off.

Plan 'A' worked to the dot. The only difference was the room. When this whole thing goes down, he [Dalrymple] scoops up Elian. For some reason, he runs into Lazaro's room, and that is where I found them.

After five months of waiting and the intensity of the early morning situation, how do you walk away from it?

I'm still coming down. I'm still very tired. Very, very, very tired. When I go through the scene in the room, it hit me real bad. This kid was crying. In a different way than kids cry. I have four kids. I know how kids cry. This wasn't the cry of a kid who wasn't feeling well or was just a pain in the butt. This was a different cry. It was lousy to be there.

I'd been shooting that kid for months. A happy kid. To see the kid in that situation really hit me. I felt bad.

Five days later, I went back. No cameras. Just to say hello.

David Guttenfelder
The people are really the story

David Guttenfelder is an AP photographer based in Tokyo after a long stint in Africa.

"When you first move to a place, it takes you a long time to learn how the people, how the culture, will react to you as a photographer," he says. "There's a certain style you develop that is consistent with the way the people are."

According to Guttenfelder, there's a big difference in the way you work in each place and some of that difference affects his shooting style and the look of his pictures.

"In Africa," he says, "the kind of style I had was very close, and the way I approached people was more aggressive. Maybe I was closer to them," he says, "maybe I could work longer on a photo

close to somebody."

Guttenfelder says his style there was very personal, "because that's the way the people are. They are more aggressive, their spaces are tight, the people are very close."

Not only did his pictures reflect that, but Guttenfelder says he noticed the same closeness in the pictures taken by other photographers working the same stories he was on in Africa. "They look like that because you start to take pictures like they (the people) are, like their culture is because that is what they allow you to do."

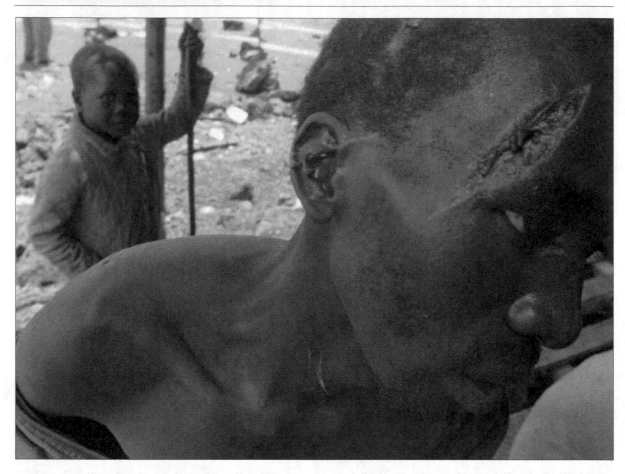

That in-your-face style doesn't work in Asia, he says.

"When you move to a place like Asia," he explained, "that approach doesn't work anymore because their culture is different. They react to you very differently."

In Japan, Guttenfelder has noted that the people are very private. "People tend not to make eye contact with strangers," Guttenfelder says, "and if they don't like being photographed, they won't tell you no. They'll just make it difficult for you by moving away or covering their face."

In Africa, he says, "if they don't like it, they will tell you! So there you feel if you have made the first frame you can make the second frame."

But he knows now that Asia is very, very different. "What you have to do is completely rethink the way you make pictures," Guttenfelder says, "the way you interact with people, and, as a result, your pictures start to look different."

After a few months in his new assignment, Guttenfelder thinks he is developing a style that will work in his new surroundings. "I am starting to make pictures that say something," he says, "and pictures that work. But they are different than I made in Africa."

He thinks eventually he'll know more about the culture and feel more comfort-

AP photographer David Guttenfelder sees a remarkable difference between his coverage of refugees in Africa and Japan in his choice of lenses and how he shoots his pictures. In Africa, Guttenfelder's approach is to work very close to the subject, often with a wide angle lens. In Asia, he finds you have to stand back a bit and use longer lenses.

able. "I'll be able to make the kind of pictures I want, and I'll be able to get close to the people," he says.

Guttenfelder considers himself something of an expert on refugee situations, having covered those kinds of stories all over Africa and in Albania as well. "I have spent more time taking pictures in refugee camps than in any other place in the last six years," he says.

But, he found it was completely different to cover refugees from a volcano in northern Japan. "Taking pictures of the Japanese refugees was fascinating for me because there were so many" differences between them and other refugees he had covered in the past. "Just in the way people react to you as a photographer and the life that people live and what's important to them," he says.

Despite the different setting, Guttenfelder felt he still was able to make important pictures by, in one respect, working the way he has in the past and which has been very successful for him.

That approach is to concentrate on the people, not in this case, the volcano. Guttenfelder says so many times he has seen photographers get caught up in the action of a war, or a natural disaster and forget that it is the people who are really the story.

David Longstreath
You're in the business to make pictures, not excuses

Have you ever sat in an airport watching the planes come and go?

AP photographer David Longstreath has dozens and dozens of times. Always with his camera bag at his side.

That paid off for him at the Phnom Penh airport, when, while waiting for a flight home to Bangkok after covering a story, he saw a passenger plane careen into a rice paddy at the edge of the airfield.

The shock of seeing an airliner crash was like seeing "a human tornado," Longstreath says. "The shock of seeing it crash. It was a tremendous fireball. There was no doubt in my mind there would be no survivors."

"It took me a minute or so to rush out the door and throw myself into the back of a fire truck. It was still burning when I got there," Longstreath says.

"It takes all of your emotions, like someone kicking you in the stomach," he says. "It just takes your breath away."

"You cannot believe what sixty-five people slaughtered in a rice paddy looks like

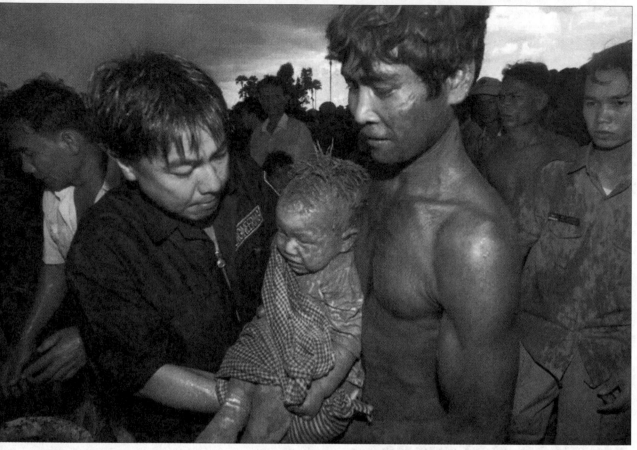

While waiting for a flight from the Phnom Penh airport, David Longstreath of the AP was faced with a tremendous challenge — a passenger airliner crashed on the outskirts of the airfield. Longstreath had his cameras and his laptop computer with him, though, so he was ready to work. His coverage included scenes of destruction but it also had the happy moment as rescue workers pulled a young baby alive from the burning wreckage and raced it away to a hospital (above).

until you see it. It is truly one of the most incredible sights I have ever witnessed."

This from a veteran photographer who was at the scene of the Oklahoma City bombing minutes after the federal building there was leveled.

Fighting back his emotions at the scene of the Phnom Penh crash, Longstreath began to make pictures. "At some point," he says, "your reflexes kick in and you've got to work and you've got to make images. You've got to make the kind of images that have a degree of sensitivity and sense of urgency and sense of compassion."

These reactions were almost automatic for Longstreath. "They are just gut reactions at this point," he says. "You don't go about it like a shopping list of a wide shot and what have you."

In the midst of all of the carnage, Longstreath heard shouts and turned and looked. A rescuer was holding a small baby in the air. The child would turn out to be the only survivor of the crash. "They start-

ed running with this kid," Longstreath says, "and I put myself in a position where I could make pictures. When they went by me, it was obvious I was only going to be able to make a couple of frames, and I wouldn't be able to chase them" because the muddy rice paddy made it difficult to go far without falling.

Longstreath thought for a moment about the images he had and decided the most important thing he could do next would be to get to a phone to alert the AP desk in Tokyo to the crash and then to transmit his pictures.

"I just grabbed a kid on a motorbike, shoved a $20 in his hand and yelled,

'Go!'" The bike rider took Longstreath to the airport terminal, where there would be phones.

"It was just one of those days when, later, all of those emotions of having witnessed something like this, it all comes out when you have time to think about it." Later, Longstreath says, "is when you have time to reflect on what you've seen, what you've been involved in. At the time, you run on reflex, you run just as fast as you can."

That drive is the hallmark of a world-class photojournalist. In this case, as always with Longstreath, he was ready to cover the action.

What if his cam-

Spectators gather around the wreckage at the crash site of a passenger airliner at the Phnom Penh airport, a day after the 1998 crash. What started as a boring wait for a flight turned into days of coverage of the crash for photographer David Longstreath.

eras had been safely stowed in a shipping case in the belly of the plane he was to catch later? What if he hadn't had his laptop with him so he could transmit?

"If you are in the business," Longstreath says, "you have to become accustomed to the notion that you are going to be carrying some kind of camera, at least the bare essentials, with you all of the time. You never know where or when the next story is going to break."

After all, Longstreath says, what would he have said to his editors if he had checked his gear and couldn't cover that crash?

"You're in the business to make pictures," he says, "not in the business to make excuses."

Charles Rex Arbogast
Doing your homework pays off

AP photographer Charles Rex Arbogast does his homework when it comes to access. In one case, he spent a couple of years working to get the inside track.

Arbogast, who covers state politics from his base in Trenton, N.J., started working on getting access to Bill Bradley while Bradley was a senator and was discussing making a run for the presidency.

That work paid off a few years later when Bradley mounted his campaign. Arbogast was able to make pictures other photographers couldn't and had access to Bradley that even some of his staff didn't have.

It was all based on the trust built up by Arbogast in those early years before Bradley became a national figure.

Arbogast began his coverage the year Bradley decided to step down from his U.S. Senate seat. "It was important to be first to do the story on the retiring senator," Arbogast says. He wanted to get his pictures in the state's newspapers but he also wanted to make an impression on Bradley and "set the stage  for later coverage of him as he was being touted for a possible presidential bid."

Photographer Charles Rex Arbogast of the AP had lived in the Seattle area before and was aware of the fish-catching ritual at the city's Pike Street market. So when presidential candidate Bill Bradley visited the market during a 2000 campaign stop, Arbogast knew where he needed to be to make the best possible picture.

Then, between the time Bradley retired from the Senate and the time he formally decided to make a bid for the presidency, Arbogast says, "I would go to events where he was at and see him privately and keep putting the bug in his ear that I wanted to be a part of the coverage of his campaign."

Sometimes there were setbacks, but Arbogast kept working at it. "One frustration was over those years new people would come on [to Bradley's staff] who you needed to convince that you needed access to Bradley," Arbogast says. "As new

people came on board, I had to prove myself all over again to people I hadn't met that my time with Bradley was important."

That work and continuing contact with Bradley paid off. When Bradley began running for the presidency in earnest and the primary season got going, Arbogast was assigned by the AP to cover him. Now was the time when all of that work would prove to be worthwhile.

Arbogast was able to make pictures behind the scenes or from angles and situations that provided a rare glimpse into the

Back in the early days of the campaign, before federal agents provided security and transport, candidate Bill Bradley would drive himself to a local gym for a workout. As the campaign continued and Bradley mixed with voters on a Seattle ferry, or took a moment alone or with his wife, photographer Charles Rex Arbogast would be there, often getting access to quiet moments away from the ordinary campaign coverage. That access came only after years of groundwork by Arbogast.

inner workings of a campaign. And, Bradley himself was the reason Arbogast got through a door or into a good spot.

"Although a handler might keep me from going through a door, once I was in the door and Bradley knew I was there, I was able to stay," Arbogast says. "They also knew the power of the AP to let me be there. Bradley was comfortable and it worked out well for the AP."

Even when the campaign hit rocky times, and Bradley's hopes faded, Arbogast still was able to make pictures. But, at the same time, "when I noticed it to be touchy in private situations, in order not to jeopardize more important future private moments, I made a judgment call to leave," he says. "I was asked to leave several times, twice by

Bradley, more times by his handlers."

But, more times than not, when Arbogast really needed to be somewhere to make a picture, he got his access. Those years of doing his homework paid off. Right to the end of the campaign.

One of Arbogast's favorite pictures from his coverage of Bradley is a picture made of the former senator driving his well-used car by himself to his campaign headquarters after his candidacy ended and Secret Service protection was lifted.

Arbogast took Bradley's offer of a lift and the two talked about a wide range of things as they made the drive. After all, he might run again and Arbogast knows moments like that will pay off over the long haul.

David Guttenfelder
Working in a human storm

David Guttenfelder's way of covering events could apply to any photographer anywhere, though on a slightly different scale.

"Sometimes when you are doing a story and you are looking for a feature picture," he explains, "you'll stumble across five guys doing a culture dance or something and you'll think you've struck gold. You'll shoot four rolls of film."

"Another time," he continues, "you'll be standing in a road with a million refugees and you don't know what to photograph." Guttenfelder says you find that you keep walking, "first a mile, then two, then three and you haven't taken any photos yet. It is overwhelming."

The photographer found himself in just that situation a few years ago while covering the refugee camps along the Rwandan border.

"Every day, we tried to go there, and we couldn't. The road was mined and they stopped us. Then, one day, we came to the top of this hill and we saw a million people coming toward us."

"For the first hour, I didn't shoot very much," he says. "I didn't know what to shoot. There is so much happening."

Finally, he realized that he had to abandon his search for the one storytelling photo and begin to chronicle the incredible exodus. "You just have to start taking pictures. If you keep walking, looking for the one photo that can possibly match the emotions you are feeling, then you might not take any."

"When you get back," he says, "you'll be surprised to discover that many of the little moments and many of the overall pictures do the job. They do tell the story."

When you're in the middle of a human storm, though, it is easy to lose track of time.

"That day," Guttenfelder says, "seemed to go on forever. You could have stood in one place and shot pictures for ninety-six hours. But, you had to pull away, you had to decide, you had to focus on what pictures would tell the story and you had to get those photos."

The assignment lasted three days. Each day, Guttenfelder would drive to where the refugees were on the road and begin his coverage. "We were going back and forth. Run out, take pictures, come back and send

pictures. Go back again." After returning to the hotel at night, he would transmit his photos and then collapse in exhaustion.

The contrast of his hotel accommodations and the misery of the refugees did wear on Guttenfelder. "You are standing there with a $2,000 lens," he says, "which is more than that person could earn in a lifetime. You have to understand. You have to believe that you are there for a reason and that what you are doing is of use to those people."

You don't leave those emotions behind when you leave, he says.

"I go home sometimes to the United States and it gives me a little perspective on what other people think are problems."

And, on those trips home, it takes a day or two to shift gears. "You ruin a lot of dinner parties with what you think is a normal conversation. I bring up a topic of conversation and everyone looks at me like I'm a madman."

David Martin
"You have to get wet to get the best pictures"

AP photographer David Martin has a pretty simple way to tell if you're covering a storm correctly.

"You have to get wet to get the best pictures," he says.

The Montgomery, Ala., based photographer should know. He's a veteran of countless hurricanes and tornadoes and he's gotten wet plenty of times and brought back good pictures, too.

Once, when forecasters initially said a hurricane was due to come ashore near Miami, Martin was there waiting for it. But the storm changed its path and headed north along the coast. Martin took off in pursuit. Eventually, Martin and the hurricane met up on the Outer Banks of North

Carolina. But, that's another story for another time.

When a hurricane hit Key West a few years ago, Martin was plenty close enough.

But that didn't happen by accident.

Editors in New York had sent him to the end of the Florida Keys because weather forecasters were predicting that's where the storm would first hit land. Equipped with the old sneakers he keeps in the garage just for storms like this, Martin headed out.

When he got to Key West, he quickly

Key West residents fight wind and rain as they make their way past houses being swept out to sea by Hurricane Georges in 1998. Photographer David Martin has a couple of rules for making good storm pictures — pictures with people in them are going to be better and you have to get wet to get the best pictures. In this image, he scored on both counts.

began gathering information. "Where does it flood? Where do people go to watch the storm," he asked the locals. Armed with the information, he knew where he wanted to be when the storm hit.

"I had a pretty good idea of where to go," he says. "We knew the storm was going to hit that side of the island." After a quick inspection trip of the area, Martin was sure he was in the right spot. "You just knew those houses were going to go."

Finding the right spot, checking out the angles, seeing if there is someplace low, or high, to get a different look -- all of these things add up to being ready.

As the storm came ashore, Martin and a

reporter went out two times to the area, but the water wasn't very high yet. Finally, on the third pass through the area, he knew he was in the middle of it. He was getting wet.

"We couldn't see the lines in the road anymore, so we knew the water was starting to get deep," he explains.

Martin made a few pictures but felt he didn't have a good one yet, because he didn't have any people in the picture. Rule two of the Martin storm code: "A picture of damage without the human element is boring. Very few of them will be successful."

About that time, Martin looked up the

road and "out of the mist came these three people who were going to ride out the storm. That all by itself was an image."

Martin stuck with them and, the wetter he got, the better the pictures got.

"I walked with them as they passed the devastated houses. The wind was blowing like hell, the water was calf deep. It was an intense moment," Martin recalls.

Martin kept his camera, equipped with a wide-angle lens, under his coat until he knew he could make a good picture.

"As they walked past the house being tossed up on the shore, that's when I fired off six or seven frames." Martin had his picture just in time. "Then the camera was too wet to do anything else."

With that, he headed in. He had his picture, with people. And he was plenty wet.

Neither chest-deep water during Hurricane Danny in Alabama in 1997 (below), nor blowing sand on a North Carolina beach in 1999 during Hurricane Dennis (right) can keep photographer David Martin away from the action.

PAYNE
STEWART
Gonna miss
You Payne
you Always
Brought Joy
to the Game
Deepest Sympathy
The Reynolds

David Phillip, Pat Sullivan
"It can get repetitive shooting flowers..."

While news coverage often tests the emotional reserves of photographers, sports photography usually requires them to pay attention while their subjects are on an emotional high or low.

AP photographer David Phillip saw one family's highs and lows during a season of golf. And felt some of that emotion himself.

Few stories in sports are as tragic as that of golfer Payne Stewart. After a career that exploded on the scene in the early 1990s, Stewart's luck turned the other way and he went years without being a serious contender. Then, in 1999, it looked like he had

it all together again.

The golfer, easily recognized on the course wearing his trademark knickers, won the U.S. Open Championship at Pinehurst, N.C., in dramatic fashion in June.

Photographer David Phillip of the AP remembers the moment quite well when Payne Stewart's putt dropped in on the final hole to give the emotive Stewart the 1999 U.S. Open title at the fabled Pinehurst course in North Carolina. Months later, Phillip would be covering the grieving and emotional followup after Stewart's chartered jet crashed in a South Dakota field and the Tour Championship tourney that week would turn into a period of mourning.

glory days and had seen the bad luck years, too.

Months went by, and although Stewart's season leveled off a bit from the high of the Open, he still was playing well and would be included in the annual Tour Championship, an event in Houston that features the top money winners of the season. Phillip was going to cover that tourney, too.

Then, while covering a trial outside Houston, Phillip overheard other journalists talking about a plane that was in trouble. "I was standing outside the courthouse and heard reports there was a plane off course flying across the country," he says. There was no word on who was on board and Phillip paid only passing attention to the story.

A couple of hours later, word came that Stewart, who had been en route from his

Phillip, who has been covering golf for several years and counts several majors, including the Masters and Open, in his credits, was happy to see Stewart win. While growing up in Dallas, where Stewart had gone to school, Phillip had followed his career. He had seen him during his

Orlando home to Dallas and then to Houston for the tourney, had been on the plane. He was killed when it crashed into a South Dakota field after running out of fuel.

"I was shocked," Phillip says. "I thought back to the Open instantly. I thought back to his comments after the tourney about being at peace in his life." Phillip thought about those comments, at such a happy moment in Stewart's life, and the events of the day. He found he was "flashing back to pictures of Stewart and his wife embracing. I thought of his children. How tragic to lose your father in a bizarre circumstance like that."

The story now was shifting to Houston, to the course where the upcoming tourncy would be played. Phillip finished up at the trial quickly and drove directly to the golf course, arriving about sunset. "There was a very somber feeling around there. A lot of people in shock. Some people had started to leave flowers." Phillip looked around, found the beginnings of a makeshift shrine at the reserved parking space which had been assigned to Stewart in anticipation of his arrival and went to work. "That's when I made the first pictures," he says. "Someone had left a note about how much they would miss him and how much he had brought to the game."

Phillip is a golfer himself and looks forward to covering the sport. But there was no joy in the assignment. It was a sad time for players, spectators and others who had seen Stewart in action over the years.

The coverage moved into a new day, and Phillip faced the dilemma often felt by photographers. He had to find a new way to tell the story.

"Obviously, it can get repetitive shooting flowers in a parking spot," he says. "I'd check periodically with tournament officials to see what they had planned. I also spent a lot of time out by the driving range and putting green where the players are more likely to talk about things, let their guard down a little." Stewart had been a popular player and the players were visibly upset, Phillip says.

He also looked for other ways to tell the story. People were starting to wear black ribbons so he sought out the source and made a picture of them being prepared. Flags were at half-staff, and Phillip checked to see who was doing that and when he could photograph that, too.

On the morning of the first round of the tourney, a memorial service was held at the

Players saluted Stewart by wearing his trademark knickers (top), fans, officials and competitors all wore black ribbons of grief (above) and tourney winner Tiger Woods saluted Stewart at the trophy presentation (left). It was a difficult week for players like Tom Lehman (opposite) who cried openly at a memorial service. Photographer David Phillip had to be alert to all of the possibilities for photos so they didn't all begin to look alike.

course. A heavy misty fog covered the course. "It was very eerie. When we got out there that morning, it was the thickest fog I had seen in a while. How fitting," Phillip says.

Phillip was working with colleague Pat Sullivan. They talked it over, and, he explains, "we took opposite angles to make sure we had all of our bases covered. I had gotten out there early and looked over things. I had marked off three positions after talking with officials. I had the 500 mm, so it made sense for me to go down the fairway and shoot back into the crowd. Pat took a more even line with the crowd, so she could get the bagpiper walking on to the green, then back with the footprints."

Phillip's angle would put the piper in line with the crowd while Sullivan's was more isolated on the piper. "I would be able to put him in the context that he was at a memorial service, with the crowd in the background. We wanted to make sure we had both contexts covered," he says.

That kind of teamwork is important. "In most situations, you know there is going to be a must picture," Phillip says. "Then you talk about the other pictures. 'Who is going

to take the risky position? Who is going to work with a particular lens or angle?' Communications is the key. Talk it out."

And, when working in a team situation, it is important to realize that one person probably won't be able to make all of the key pictures of the day. But collectively you will have a full report.

"It was important David and I worked different angles," Sullivan says. "He had the prime spot for all of the other pictures. His overall take was much better than mine, because he had a better angle during the service."

But the piper picture from Sullivan's angle turned out to be the key image. "When I saw the footprints in the dew," she says, "I hoped he would follow the same path out. And, he did. Everything came together the way you hoped it would. That doesn't happen very often."

There is a range of topics to go over when you are working with another photographer, just as when you are working alone. "What is the key image? What is the key angle? What about this when this happens? Never assume someone else is thinking the same thing you are thinking," Phillip says. "In this business everyone has

David Phillip and colleague Pat Sullivan arrived early for a memorial service for Stewart and checked out the scene and talked with officials to see what would be happening. With that planning, they took up positions to give the greatest variety to their coverage while making sure they had the key moments, including Sullivan's dramatic view of a lone bagpiper walking off into the mist after playing "Amazing Grace."

a different eye and a different approach."

In the case of the piper picture, for Sullivan it was a matter of taking a position that normally would have been undesirable — a picture of someone's back. "This goes back to not taking things for granted," Sullivan says. "We get in the habit of shooting people's faces. In this case, it doesn't matter who the piper was. It was the symbol. To me it was more appropriate for him to be leaving."

When the day was over, Phillip and Sullivan had a good set of pictures and Phillip had the finish to the photo essay of his

memories of Payne Stewart.

"I was very touched by it all," he says. "It brought to mind him holding that trophy on the 18th green after winning the Open. I actually thought about his family and how they were doing, how they were handling his death."

For a moment, as that piper disappeared into the fog, Phillip thought of the time months before on the 18th at Pinehurst. "It was like a step back in time. We were watching that putt rolling and dropping in."

Remotes
A second way to see

Remotes are all about options.

There's the perfect angle, or view, of an event. But you can't be there while the game or meeting is under way. Or there's a secondary angle that might, or might not, pay off. But it is worth a look, that's for sure.

Unmanned cameras, fired by radio, by using a switch on the end of a hard wire, or by computers linked by microwave transmitters, let photographers be in more than one place at a time.

Hard wire, which is basic electric extension or "zip" cord, is the simplest method and most foolproof. One end has a socket which mates with the camera's remote firing arrangement. The other has a simple hand or foot switch attached to complete the electrical circuit.

Another method is to use a radio remote.

One vendor produces a unit called the Pocket Wizard. It is a sophisticated piece of equipment that can be used to fire cameras or trip strobe lights remotely. It has a button on the sending unit, or an external switch can be used. The receiving unit mounts at the camera or strobes and plugs in the same way the hard wire setup operates.

That's the setup AP photographer David Phillip uses. "It is a relatively easy setup and it doesn't take a lot of time to do it. You can keep all of your gear in one bag," he says. Phillip uses Velcro to attach the

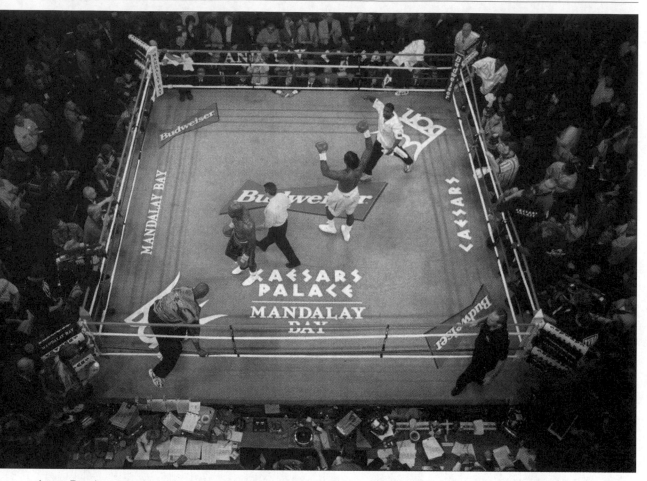

Laura Rauch mounted a camera on a light boom over the ring at the 1999 Holyfield-Lewis heavyweight bout in Las Vegas (above); Mike Conroy used a remote mounted behind the backboard glass for this view of a 1999 San Antonio-New York NBA Finals game (opposite, top), and David Phillip routinely mounts a remote camera for an extra shot at plays at the plate while covering the Astros in Houston (opposite, bottom).

receiving unit to the camera clamp and a foot switch to fire it.

Phillip first started using remotes by stringing out hard wire. "When I first started using them, I would have 500 feet of zip cord spread around a basketball court. It was pretty messy cleaning up after the game with all of the beer and Coke spilled on them." He was a lot happier when he switched to using radio remotes. "It is so easy," he says.

There is one thing to watch, Phillip says, when using the radio remotes. Others using the same units can inadvertently trip your camera if they are on the same channel. "That got to be very frustrating," Phillip says.

At big events, there often is a sign-up sheet for channels to keep this from happening. Or Phillip and other photographers take it a step further. "With the new advances in radio remotes, I have had custom channels installed [in his radios], so no one else can fire them." That is a quick and relatively inexpensive fix for the problem.

The third method to fire remote cameras is a new product just making its debut in remote setups. Nikon and Lucent Technologies have teamed up to develop a hardware/software solution that fires a digital camera linked by a short cable to a laptop. It then

sends that image file over microwave radio frequencies to another laptop. The two laptops are not linked by any wires and can be quite a distance apart and not necessarily in sight of each other. A person at the receiving end fires the camera by hitting the space

bar on the laptop keyboard instead of by using external switches.

Earlier methods from other vendors required someone to manually transmit the images. And the sending and receiving stations had to be in line of sight with each other.

Phillip is a regular user of remotes. "I think it is a great advantage," he says. "It is worth any time and effort. The advantage you gain from a second position is well worth it."

That can mean setting up a camera in the third base photo position at a baseball game while you are in the first base box. Or in an overhead position when you are at first or third. Some photographers even leave a remote set up when they leave the field to transmit their images. If they see a play at the plate happening on their workroom television, they hit the remote switch.

Any way you do it, the remote gives you another chance to get the picture you want. Phillip rigs up a remote looking at home plate from an alternate position at most of the baseball games he goes to. Plays at the plate, he says, are the most unpredictable and yield the most return in terms of telling the story. "You never know how the player is going to slide into the plate or how the play might go," Phillip says. "The remote gives me a chance to make sure I have a picture when I'm covering a game alone." He says the effort is worth it. "It has paid off quite a bit. If I set it up ten games in a row, I'll get two or three pictures from it," he says. "It can make a big difference in my coverage."

Remotes also can provide a supplemental picture to the photographer's take from an event, often a secondary picture that helps round out the story.

In the White House, AP photographer Doug Mills has used a remote camera in a doorway to show President Bill Clinton coming or going from a briefing. The picture helps break up the standard podium coverage that is driven by the control exercised over photographers' movements covering the president. And it gives some atmos-

News assignments can be better covered by using remotes, too. Doug Mills mounted a camera over a doorway to catch a different picture of President Bill Clinton leaving an East Room news conference in 1997.

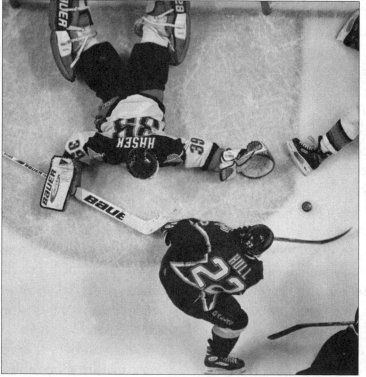

Using a remote camera mounted on a walkway in the ceiling of the arena, Gene Puskar's picture of Brett Hull scoring the winning goal in the 1999 Stanley Cup finals title game showed Hull's skate in the crease which should have negated the goal.

phere to what can be a sterile setting.

At a Stanley Cup finals playoff game in Buffalo, Gene Puskar of the AP used a remote camera mounted on a catwalk in the arena ceiling to provide a different view of plays around the goal. That angle paid off even more than expected when Brett Hull of the Dallas Stars scored the winning goal in overtime, giving the 1999 Stanley Cup to the Stars. Puskar had the frame.

The goal was controversial. Sabres players and coaches claimed Hull's skate was inside the crease, the protected area around the goaltender, when he scored. This would have disallowed the goal. As you might imagine, Hull and the Stars were quiet on the subject after National Hockey League officials ruled the goal good.

But Puskar's picture showed Hull's skate clearly within the line and Sabres fans had it to study and grumble about over the long summer after they lost the championship.

Remotes work well in basketball, too. A camera was clamped to the backboard support behind the glass by Mike Conroy of the AP during a 1999 NBA Finals game in San Antonio. The remote camera gave Conroy a picture from a vantage point where no photographer could actually work during a game. And, after a long season of pictures from the floor up, it also provided a different angle.

AP photographer Laura Rauch mounted a remote on a light boom over a boxing ring to make a telling picture of boxer Lennox Lewis heading back to his corner with his arms raised in victory as his fight with Evander Holyfield ended. It is a clean view that would have been difficult to

make from any other angle.

And, in soccer, the key action is going to be near the net in most instances. AP photographer Mark Terrill placed a remote at

Mark Terrill mounted a camera in the back of the goal to capture this dramatic photo of Chinese goalie Hong Gao making an unsuccessful save attempt on the winning overtime shootout kick in the 1999 women's World Cup match won by the U.S. squad.

the back of the net to get China's goalie, Hong Gao, missing the kick in overtime which gave the United States the women's World Cup title. The low angle and Gao's stretching form give the picture its punch.

For Mills, Conroy, Rauch and Terrill, a remote camera gave them pictures from places they couldn't be themselves. In the cases of Puskar and Phillip, remotes gave them the chance to cover two angles at once.

Either way, the versatility remotes afford makes them worth the effort.

Lighting:
Using Light to Your Advantage

Lighting for photojournalism can be as complex as a multiple-strobe operation or as simple as exposing your film properly on a sunny day.

But the secret seems to be to use light, whatever the source, and make it work for you.

When slugger Mark McGwire was racing to break Roger Maris' home run record, AP photographer Ed Reinke used available light.

And, he used a flash, actually hundreds of them, to make a dramatic point with a picture. They weren't his flashes, though. They were the flashes from the cameras of fans making pictures when McGwire came to the plate.

"That was a picture we had all seen on television," Reinke says. "Television had made so much of it. In the ballparks from Florida to Cincinnati to St. Louis, we had seen still photographers make attempts at it and end up with two flashes in the picture. I thought about it and thought about it and thought about it," he says. "I went back to my room and watched it on ESPN and thought, 'Wow, there are a lot of flashes.'"

The next night, Reinke thought he had it figured out. He decided to give it a try but he hadn't gathered the necessary equipment. So he improvised. He put the camera on the concrete apron in front of his photo

Opposite page: Ed Reinke of the AP made one frame, a keeper, of hundreds of flashes going off with St. Louis Cardinals slugger Mark McGwire at bat as he chased the home run record in 1998.

position. "I put the PCMCIA gloves [small cases for digital camera disks] under the lens of the camera and set it on 2.5 seconds and stopped it down and thought, 'I'm going to give this a try his first at-bat.' He's swinging for 61."

"I poked the button as the pitch came," Reinke says, "and I am trying to handhold the 300 with my other hand. I gave it one try and said to myself, 'That's it, I'm not going to take the chance if he hits this thing.' If he had hit it just then, as it turns out I would have been golden. But I wasn't going to take the chance any more."

The picture was a winner, even if it wasn't made at the most significant moment of the night. "I can't say I was very prepared to do it," Reinke says. "But I knew exactly what I wanted to accomplish. I was mentally prepared, but I wasn't physically prepared. I made one frame and it worked."

Reinke had dozens of flashes in his picture and it turns out he was successful because, for just a moment, he stopped thinking like a photographer and thought more as a fan. And, a fan more times than not would react to the pitch rather than anticipate it as a photographer would.

"Timing is so much of that. Most of the people that missed it [the flashes] were thinking more like a photographer than a spectator. In fact, the ball is in the catcher's mitt. Of the 55,000 fans in Busch Stadium who were trying to make a picture of him hitting his 61st home run, I doubt there

were three who had the ball coming off the bat which is what we (photographers) strive for."

Reinke had seen the light, as it were, and used it to his advantage.

Rusty Kennedy tells of the guidance he got from a veteran photographer at the former *Philadelphia Bulletin* when just starting out. The veteran told Kennedy, "Don't just look at your light meter, look at your light. Look at it, look at how it falls."

To illustrate a story on the emergence of new high-intensity car lights, AP photographer Robert Bukaty shot the car in a darkened area with the headlights on and used a strobe below and behind the car to backlight and outline the scene.

Kennedy says that "because meters are so accurate now, sometimes photographers don't look at the light," and they lose a lot of feeling in their pictures when they don't let light work for them.

When available light isn't sufficient, or actually hinders a good exposure, photographers shouldn't be reluctant to use auxiliary light, which they provide themselves. That can range from small flash units to larger multiple head strobe arrays or photo flood kits.

It doesn't have to be anything complex to be helpful. Eric Risberg explains, "I had a chance to work with Mark Kauffman, the former Life photographer. I worked with him for two months and he taught me about lighting, from simple assignments to how to light a building."

Risberg says the most important thing Kauffman taught him was that, "you don't need a lot of lighting equipment to make good pictures."

Understanding your equipment will help you stretch its usefulness. "Being a photojournalist," Indianapolis freelancer Mary Ann Carter says, "you have to be adaptable and know what your tools are going to do. A strobe, an umbrella, a softbox or the ability to push film are just that, tools to be used when they are needed."

"You have to look at the light that is there," Carter says, "and figure out what is going to work in that situation. What worked today, won't always work tomorrow. What worked on chromes, might not work in black and white photography."

Carter says, "The best thing to do is to practice with your tools, one foot from the subject, five feet from the subject. Learn what the light does, what it doesn't do."

Doug Pizac of the AP says those practice sessions can reveal a lot. Approach them with several objectives in mind so you can get the most information about your equipment.

For instance, check the falloff of light from your strobe equipment so you'll know how it will light scenes with various lens. Pizac says, for example, some strobes

AP photographer Eric Draper made good use of a strobe coupled with a device to spread the light to give an overall even exposure to this wide angle view of presidential candidate George W. Bush early in 2000.

will easily cover the field of a 35 mm lens but cautions that using a 24 mm lens with that same strobe will produce falloff, the edges will get less light than the central area.

Adapters are available to spread the light, but Pizac says there are some instances where the falloff helps. If you're working in a crowded hallway, for instance, like a news assignment outside a courtroom where people are on either side of the subject, but closer to the photographer, Pizac says, "use a 24 mm lens with no attachment on the strobe. The subject will be properly illuminated," and the "light falloff from the strobe will be enough to correctly expose the people on the fringe since they are closer to the light source."

If you're going to be doing a great deal of lighting, Carter suggests a couple of items that will help you gain the best quality from your lighting equipment.

She finds a flash meter, which measures both strobe and ambient light, to be extremely helpful when setting up lighting units that don't have automatic exposure controls.

Another tool she uses is a press camera with a special back that takes Polaroid film so you have "instant" feedback on your lighting.

Carter says, "I find it helpful because it tells me when I have a reflection that I don't want, or if I'm throwing a shadow that is awkward. It's not for determining exposure, that's what I use the flash meter for, but it's for looking at relationships in the picture."

"It gives you a sneak preview of what is going to be on the film. If there is a glaring error, it will show you where it is," she says.

Wyatt Counts, a freelance photographer based in New York, also uses the Polaroid method to check his lighting. With the Polaroid, he says, "You get some idea of what your light is doing before you commit it to film."

Photographer Wyatt Counts used a softbox to take the harshness out of a strobe light in this thoughtful 1990 study of rock guitarist Eric Clapton.

He also uses the Polaroids to smooth over any fears his subjects might have. If a subject seems nervous, Counts will make a quick exposure on the Polaroid film and give it to them "so they can see you're serious about it and making them look good." That usually relaxes them.

Counts also uses a Hawk remote system. It's a radio device to fire his strobes. It frees him from having wires running all over the place, "where people can trip over them," he says. And, it allows him to put the strobes in places where it might be difficult to run a wire.

Just as you have to pay attention to your lighting, you have to pay attention to your equipment, too. Pizac says not to forget to check the calibration of your various meters, both in the camera and the hand-held flash meter. He suggests shooting tests, carefully recording the data, then evaluating the film to see where there might be discrepancies. Also you should check for situations that might fool the meter, or the photographer.

"A meter is only a guide," Pizac warns, "a starting point. Look at what the meter says and interpret the reading. Do not rely on it."

It's important to learn what lighting can do for you.

The simplest lighting exercise, which calls for the least amount of equipment, is flash fill. That involves using a strobe to fill shadow areas in a sun-lit scene.

A rule of thumb for flash fill is to set your automatic strobe, or calculate your strobe to subject distance on a manual unit, to produce one stop less light than the existing light exposure.

For instance, if the existing light is f11, the fill flash should produce light at f8. This way, the "fill" light will open up the shadows while the "natural" light will still be dominate and the scene will retain its natural appearance.

You'll need a camera that synchs at a 250th of a second, or faster, to make easy use of the flash-fill technique. It's difficult without shifting to extremely slow speed

Mark Duncan of the AP used fill flash to negate bothersome shadows under the bill of the cap worn by racing driver Bobby Rahal on a sunny day at the 1996 Cleveland Grand Prix.

films to use flash fill outdoors with a camera that synchs at a 60th of a second or slower.

Flash fill will give you an immediate quality boost and make your negatives more easily printable without having to do extensive dodging in the underexposed eye sockets, or extensive burning on overexposed areas while fighting to retain detail in the shadows.

Using a slower speed film, such as an ASA100 or ASA200 stock, will let you open up the aperture and cut down on the depth of field.

Carter explains how fill flash helps when shooting in the open pit area at the Indianapolis Motor Speedway. "At the track, I'm trying to get some light up under the baseball caps that everyone wears, and I want the background to come up normal, so I make the flash a stop less than the overall exposure."

She says, "It's a matter of balancing out the light. If I'm exposing for the ambient light at a 250th at f8, I'll shoot the flash at f5.6. And, I can shoot the flash on camera because the sun wipes out the negative aspects of doing that."

Carter also uses flash fill in other situations.

For a magazine client, she needed a portrait of the co-speakers of the Indiana House of Representatives with the Capitol dome behind them. The only time they could do it was in the late afternoon, and the only place to shoot the picture from was a parking garage roof that would leave the subjects extremely back-lit.

"In order to make the picture work, I had to light them," Carter explains. "And, to make the subjects stand out, I didn't want the background to be overexposed. I had to put a lot of light on the fronts of the subjects so that the background would be a normal exposure, or a little underexposed. It had a nice effect because the sun gave a rim light to the subjects and my light gave their faces detail and made the exposure work."

Pizac used fill flash to improve the quality of a picture he made of a peregrine falcon on a 26th-floor window ledge. The picture was made to go with a story on the "urbanization" of the bird.

To separate the falcon from the harsh, cross-lit background, Pizac used an extremely wide aperture to cut down on the depth of field. Then, he set his strobe, using the unit's variable power option, to fire at extremely low power. The strobe

Photographer Doug Pizac of the AP had a different kind of subject in this 1989 portrait of a peregrine falcon on the ledge of an L.A. office building, but the challenge to expose the picture correctly was one Pizac had faced before. He used the same kind of solution he would use on a human — fill flash.

filled in the shadows under the bird's body and put some "catch" lights in its eyes.

It's not your everyday assignment, but a good example of how watching the lighting and using fill flash can improve your work.

The other basic lighting concept to learn is the use of "bounce" lighting to soften the effect of the strobe.

It gets its name from exactly what it is, a method where you "bounce" the strobe's output off a surface, usually a ceiling, to spread the light and cut the harsh shadows produced by the strobe. Bouncing the strobe light gives your pictures a more natural look, while still giving you the quality of a strobe-lit picture.

To bounce the strobe light, point the flash tube at the object (the ceiling in most cases) you'll use as a reflector, being careful to point the strobe's exposure sensor at the subject if you're using an automatic unit.

Hold the strobe so three or four of your fingers act as a small reflector to "kick" some of the strobe's output directly at your subject. Or, you can use a caption card or small piece of white cardboard, attached with tape or a rubber band to the strobe.

This will give you the brighter fill you'll want to lighten the eye sockets on your subject and provide a highlight, without hitting the subject with the full effect of the strobe light.

Bouncing the strobe light takes some practice, but is a pleasing lighting effect. Your pictures won't look lit but will have a more pleasing tonal range without deep shadows.

two photographers, Pizac and AP photographer Harry Cabluck.

Old photography and lighting manuals are a good source of information. Pizac says one of his favorites is titled, "1001 Ways To Improve Your Photographs." The 1945 book, Pizac says, "is a treasure chest of information. The photos themselves may appear dated, but the techniques themselves are everlasting."

He says grab one if you ever see it. He gets to look at one that's in his uncle's collection of photo books.

Bouncing the light from her strobe off the ceiling, AP photographer Amy Sancetta was able to get a more workable exposure in the tight confines of a bathroom in this imaginative portrait of a young girl who had written in an essay, "I am curious about what my dad talks to himself about in the shower."

Pizac does have a collection of old texts from the '40s and '50s, case studies on lighting from the Paramount and MGM studios, and he says those provide good examples to follow. "Go for those books and get back to the basics," Pizac says, adding that older town libraries often have these books on the shelves. "You've just got to search them out."

One warning if you're shooting color images: Watch the color of the surface you're bouncing your light off. The strobe will pick up that color and your subject will be "lit" with the colored light. Try to bounce off neutral surfaces for this reason.

Getting back to basics is the message of

AP photographer Mark Duncan adds another source for lighting ideas. "I get a lot of my ideas from looking at non-journalistic types of pictures to see how they use light, like corporate reports and industrial pictures."

Pizac says an important reason for being careful in lighting is that it will make other parts of your job quicker and easier. "People go out and do a job, and then they

Cabluck learned his basics at the *Fort Worth Star-Telegram* in the days when film speeds were so slow you had to supplement any lighting. Cabluck looked to a two-strobe setup to put depth in his pictures. "Your subject in the foreground lit with one light, something in the background lit

Photographers have to learn to look at how to use multiple strobes and how the light is working when they are faced with a setup to shoot a series of portraits in one location. This trio of headshots, by photographer Mary Ann Carter, shows some simple rules to follow to achieve high quality. The hairlight on the subjects at center and left provide separation. But, the subject at right would show a reflection if the hairlight was used so it was cut off for his sitting. And, the lens aperture was opened a half-stop for the left subject to give uniform densities in the exposures. This set of pictures shows there is no single way that will work in every situation.

spend an hour preparing the finished image. If they had shown more care when shooting, the printing or scanning would have been completed in far less time."

"When you make your picture," Pizac says, "you should correct the lighting so when you come in, you don't have to fool around." By working with your lighting at the assignment, you can scan your negative or acquire your digital image without having to worry about correcting for color shifts.

by another light, with the subject set off by the spill from the back light. We called it a 3D shot."

"The secret to the 3D shot is to have the best light stands you can get," Cabluck says. "If you think you need a six-foot light stand, get a twelve-footer. Get a light stand twice the length that you think you will need," so you have the greatest flexibility in placing your lights.

"And, put the camera on a tripod, even if you don't think you need to. Most news photographers probably don't use a tripod enough," Cabluck says.

Using a tripod not only makes for a steadier image when shooting at slower shutter speeds (which lets the photographer take advantage of natural light), it also gives the photographer a platform to view his scene from. The photographer then has a better chance to look through the camera and make sure the picture is composed the way he wants it.

Cabluck's simple lighting formula is to "have the lights greater than 90 degrees apart." Visualize the scene like the "subject is in the center of an imaginary circle," he says. "You don't want to have the camera centered right between the lights. One light should be aimed at the subject and one on the background with some spill over on to the subject."

Cabluck adds an important item to watch for. "The mistake most people make is to put the subject light too high." Your aim, Cabluck says, is to "not have the light so high that the nose shadow splits the lip."

An easy exposure ratio is used. "If the subject is f8, the background light would be a half a stop hotter so it would show up."

Cabluck calls the old 3D setup "a simple two-light setup that looks like three lights." Simple, but still effective for many jobs. And, by using umbrellas to soften the lighting, the setup can have a more modern look.

As part of the basics, Carter suggests starting your lighting setups from the background and moving forward. "Solve your background," she says, "then light your foreground, the subject. And keep it simple and clean."

Pizac seconds that suggestion. "Watch your background. Keep it clean, or let it work for you by enhancing the subject," he says.

"If I'm in a factory and I have this large expanse," Carter says, "I have to figure whether I'm going to let it go black, or if I want some detail, or do I want it over-exposed, or do I want it the correct color?" She says she runs through her options, asking, "What do I want it to do?"

When she knows the effect she wants, and she has lit it for that effect, she can go to her subject knowing that the background is going to work with the foreground to make a good picture.

At an assignment at the local phone company, Carter was faced with making a picture among rows of metal racks with elec-

> Using a tripod not only makes for a steadier image when shooting at slower shutter speeds (which lets the photographer take advantage of natural light), it also gives the photographer a platform to view his scene from. The photographer then has a better chance to look through the camera and make sure the picture Is composed the way he wants it.

tronic equipment. "It took a long time to solve the lighting problem," she says. "I didn't have enough light to light a whole row, and I had to make a dull picture better by using dramatic lighting, so I ended up turning the background light toward the subject." She explains that "this put some rim light on him, and parts of the background were overexposed and other parts had a dimension to them because of the backlighting."

"Then," Carter says, "I lit him from the front with an umbrella. Finally, I composed it so I didn't have to go into the dark area that I couldn't light." A simple two light solution to a tough problem.

There are other techniques and other tools.

Risberg prefers to use a "softbox" on his strobe to give himself the look of window light he wants for many of his pictures. He explains, "The softbox recreates window light, and it produces some of the most

Photographer Wyatt Counts balanced the light from his strobe with window light to give uniform density to this environmental portrait of a couple in their New York apartment.

pleasing and natural light possible from an artificial source."

Risberg also believes that using a strobe and the softbox close to the subject brings a certain look to his pictures. "I try to keep the light, the main light, as close to the subject as I can. The closer the light is to the subject, the softer it gets." Risberg warns that "a lot of photographers make the mistake of keeping their light too great a distance from their subject, but in reality the closer you get it, the softer it is when diffused by an umbrella or softbox."

Carter says you should get a feel for how the softbox or umbrella will fit in to your type of assignments. "A softbox falls off faster than an umbrella," she says, "so if you're lighting a subject and you don't want to light the background, use a softbox. But, if you want to light the background, use an umbrella because it is going to throw the light farther."

Counts believes that you can go for very different effects by using your lighting tools differently.

To strengthen a moody or sad moment in a portrait, he'll use a strobe directly on the subject and shoot it so the background goes dark. And, he'll have the subject look off camera.

For a softer effect to reinforce a more pleasant moment in a portrait, Counts will use a strobe with a softbox or umbrella. And, he'll have the subject look directly into the camera.

When shooting a portrait, Pizac sometimes uses a 4-foot-by-4-foot screen which he places between the subject and the strobe. The screen softens the light and spreads it.

For simple portraits in an office, Duncan likes to supplement the lighting in a low-key manner. Duncan says, "I tend to light all of them, put small strobes inside the lamp shades to make it look like the natur-

al light in the room." Using a small strobe to augment lighting gives Duncan the feel of available light and the quality of a studio shoot.

Photographers learn new lessons every day

Larry Nighswander: "Perseverance. Not giving up when you fail." Nighswander wanted to learn lighting so he bought four apples and worked on his technique in his apartment. "It took me five days of shooting until I got the picture I wanted. The apples were about to give up." The picture is still hanging in his office as a reminder. "If you want to strive for excellence, you don't give up. You try until you get it."

Alex Burrows: "Find the right school and get the right training. Get a good education. Not only a practical education but expand that with a general knowledge of the world and people. Then go to a newspaper that will nurture your work. You've got to find the right outlet for your work that encourages you to get better."

"If it is something that demands a more dramatic effect, I will do that, but I generally like the natural approach. You light it so the subject stands out with a softer approach." With the flash in the lamp trick, "it looks like the regular lamp but with more power."

To balance the light for the natural look, Duncan measures the available light in the room and raises it in the same proportion using the small flash units to supplement the existing light and fill the deep shadows.

It's a balance of lighting and film speed. "If I'm going to shoot only strobe, I'll try

room is preserved, but the quality and separation of the components is enhanced.

Amy Sancetta also likes to have a natural look in many of her assignments. Depending on the situation, she'll try to use natural light as a second light, perhaps lighting the background, along with a strobe.

"If I have a choice, and I can put someone in a chair near a window, I'll use it as the main source and fill in the shadow with a strobe. I'll light the person with some balanced strobe light on their face from the shadow side to give detail, but not overpower the window light."

AP photographer Doug Pizac had to work around possible reflections in the computer's screen, the need to synch his shutter speed with the monitor so as not to get a black bar on it, and the need to balance the exposure so the screen could be read while making this picture of a Web site official in his company's lab.

Sancetta thinks "natural light is so pretty. If you can use it in conjunction with flash, it can give your pictures a softer look."

to shoot only slower film, but if I'm balancing available light, I'll stick with 400 speed films."

For example, if the available light in the room is a 30th of a second at f5.6, but there are troublesome shadows, Duncan will light the shadow areas with strobes at that f5.6 exposure, then shoot the picture at a 30th. This way the natural balance of the

Like Sancetta and Duncan, Ed Reinke likes to use existing light when he can. "As much as possible, I try to work with existing light," he says. "I think it [working with or simply augmenting existing light] is more challenging than going into a studio and completely controlling the light."

"If I'm going into a CEO's office," Reinke says, "my tendency is to make that portrait by just augmenting the light that is there." And he does that by using many of the same methods that Duncan and Sancetta use.

There are specific instances in which Reinke also will use light to help tell the story. He explains, "I made a portrait of a man making a low-budget horror movie, and I controlled the environment much more tightly and used really low-level light to make him look evil, which fit in with the story."

Reinke says you need to control the light to make it work for you. "It's up to us to marry the portrait with the story," he says. "I'll shut a light off completely, or move a light, if I can make a better picture that way." He adds that he makes these changes, "just in a feature, not in news situations. Never in news. So much that we do now is feature-oriented, we can reasonably take more control."

A different kind of balance had to be achieved by photographer Wyatt Counts when he gelled his strobe to balance it with the output of the fluorescent lights in an office while making this portrait of a textile company executive. The strobe helps pop the subject out of the background while the gel prevents an annoying color shift.

Carter says turning out the room lights, and using a strobe, is the easiest way to make a good picture of someone working at a computer terminal. "The strobe has to be where it won't hit the screen, high and off to the side, facing toward the subject."

Her method involves turning off the ambient light in the room and taking a light reading, using the camera's built-in meter, off of the screen. If the screen exposure is 1/8th of a second at f8, for instance, Carter will put the camera on a tripod, set the strobe at f8, and make her exposures. The exposure of the subject and the screen will be balanced.

You can also use a strobe to freeze action, or to add an effect to a picture with movement. Carter had a magazine assignment about an exhibit at a children's museum, the science of sport. The item they wanted to feature was an angular momentum device, which involves the child, "twirling around and throwing out their arms to see if it slows them down or makes them go faster," Carter recalls.

Carter had a young volunteer working with her. "He was twirling around and I was trying different things and lots of different shutter speeds," she says. "I was trying to see if I could get the idea of this movement and still see that it was a kid."

Carter tried so many different things, and so many shutter speeds, that her first volunteer got a little queasy and had to be replaced. After finding another volunteer, she continued the assignment.

When Carter thought she had arrived at the right shutter speed, she says, "I lit it, because the flash would stop his movement so we could see clearly that it was a child on the apparatus. The strobe light was directly above him coming down and the picture combined the blur of the movement with the sharp image from the flash exposure.

To clean up the background, which was mainly other displays, Carter got up on a high ladder and used the museum's black floor as a plain backdrop. "There was even a red stripe for an accent," she says.

If you are shooting color film and using strobes to supplement existing light, inside or outside, you often face a mixture of color temperatures.

A light source's color temperature is a scientific measurement, measured in Kelvin, of the exact color of light produced by the source. For example, a strobe produces a daylight balance of 5500° Kelvin. A common household or office fluorescent might be 4500° Kelvin, while an incandescent

bulb might be 3200° Kelvin.

Obviously, if you are shooting a picture in a room that has incandescent light and you add strobe lighting, the color balance

Using the right gels

Rosco 3304, a green gel, corrects the strobe to match the fluorescent lighting.

Rosco 3308 gel converts fluorescent to daylight.

Rosco 3401 will balance with the portable lights used by television news crews.

will be off. The incandescent-lit areas will be warm — reddish — and the strobe-lit areas will be cold — bluish.

When you make a print or the engraver goes to make the separations from the chrome, only one of these shifts can be corrected.

The same problem exists when shooting in a room lit by fluorescent tubes. The fluorescent-lit areas will be green and the strobe-lit areas will have a daylight balance.

To make everything the same temperature, you can gel your strobes, so they match the available light. This way the person preparing the final image only needs to make one correction.

A popular brand is the Rosco gel. It's sold in sheets at many theatrical lighting shops and large camera stores.

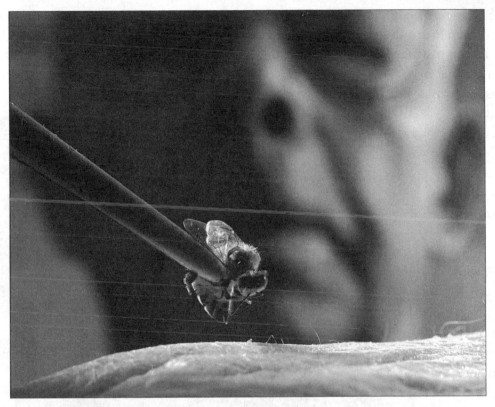

AP photographer Robert Bukaty had to keep an eye on the lighting details for both a honeybee and an arthritis sufferer. The man stings himself with bees three times a week, and has been doing it for the last 25 years to relieve his arthritis pain.

The lighting source can be as small as a kerosene lamp (above) used by AP photographer Eric Draper or as large as multiple strobes lighting an arena for the NCAA Final Four by Rich Clarkson (right).

The Rosco 3304, a green gel, corrects the strobe to match the fluorescent lighting. "When I'm in a situation with fluorescent lights in the background," Carter says, "I put those gels over the flash heads, and then put a 30 magenta filter on the lens. The gel makes all of the light fluorescent, everything will be green, then the magenta filter cleans up everything. The skin tones are true and the fluorescent lights in the background are white."

You need that magenta filter when you shoot chromes, but if you are using color negative film or shooting with a digital camera, you can go without it and correct the balance when you make the print.

If you want to filter the lights, not the strobes, the Rosco 3308 gel converts fluorescent to daylight.

You can also balance your strobe with incandescent lights. For example, the Rosco 3401 will balance with the portable lights used by television news crews. By putting a gel on your strobe, you can shoot fill flash in situations where television photographers have set up lights, or in a spot news situation where you are working among TV crews and can't control their lighting. This gel also would work in an office or home lit by regular table lamps or ceiling spots.

Knowing when to use the available light is as important as knowing how to add light. Enric Marti, of the Associated Press, used the existing light to capture this Jewish pilgrim praying near Cairo.

"The Rosco Jungle Book, a sampler of all of the corrective filters they make, is a good reference to carry in your camera bag because it tells you what each filter will do," Carter says, and will help you solve lighting-balance problems. As a bonus, she says, the sample pages will cover the head of some of the small portable strobes now in use, so you can use them right out of the book.

You also can use gels with strobes to add a dramatic effect to a picture in a feature or commercial situation.

Carter has used a gel to produce golden

sunlight on an overcast day. She had to photograph a subject in a corn field. The sun wasn't shining, and the client needed a late afternoon feeling. "I put an orange filter over the strobe in a softbox," Carter says, "and put the light to the side. It made it look like a late afternoon sun."

Others also use this technique. "I will use color gels to make a more dramatic sort of photograph when I'm not making a straight portrait of someone," Duncan says.

On one assignment involving a NASA plasma experiment, Duncan used a light red gel on a strobe to give definition to the subject and "juice it up a little bit. The assignment was done in a darkened room, with a long exposure. That showed up the plasma, and a small strobe then exposed the worker."

Another of Duncan's assignments was a portrait of a laser surgeon. He set up a

strobe to light the subject from the side with a soft light. "The strobe had a gel to give a blue highlight to outline his face and body, and he is pointing the laser at the camera."

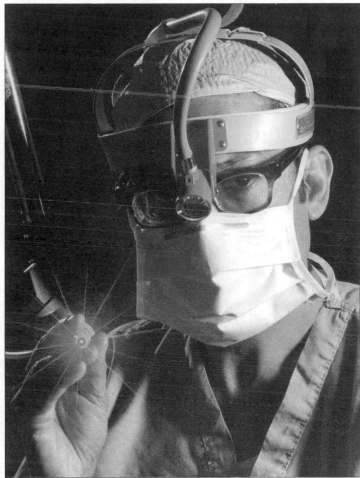

AP photographer Mark Duncan used a slow shutter speed and a small aperture to make a starburst pattern with the guide light for a laser surgery device. Duncan lit the situation from the side so he could show the laser starburst off against a dark backdrop.

Duncan shot the scene with a small aperture and slow shutter speed. The laser's guide light (a small aiming beam) is made into a star burst by the aperture of the lens. "It gave a feeling of the power of the device, since you can't actually see the laser," he says.

Duncan warns that lighting tricks such as color gels should be saved "for feature material while sticking to straight documentation for news and sports."

Carter advises there is "no one right way to light everything. But, I guess that is true of photography. There is no one right way to shoot everything."

Electronic Photography:
Pictures Without Film

From film images captured with a scanner, to digital still photography, to digital video.

After a long period with few substantive changes in photo technologies, the past ten years have been a rush through technology. And, a redefining of what a photographer does, how that photographer communicates.

Through all those changes in technology and techniques, AP photographer J. Scott Applewhite says it is important to keep the basic concepts of photojournalism in mind. "Technology changes," he says, "but our standards are rooted in the basic principals. You tell the story. You don't lie. Just the way we do it changes."

In 1988, a revolutionary device called an AP Leafax transmitter allowed a photographer to scan his processed film, instead of making a print. The photographer then could send that image to an attached receiver or transmit it over a conventional telephone line. Even then, the signal produced was still a traditional analog one and it still took ten minutes to transmit a black and white photo. A color took thirty minutes.

It was hailed as a giant step forward, allowing the photographer the freedom to work without a traditional print darkroom.

At the same time, early versions of digital cameras were being used but quality concerns, expense, and cumbersome equipment limited the usefulness.

Electronic picture terminals have moved from the bulky mainframe systems of the late '70s and '80s to the proprietary equipment of the late '80s and early '90s to the off-the-shelf solutions like this AP Server based on a standard office platform unveiled in 1999.

In the early 1990s, the Associated Press installed electronic darkrooms in newsrooms around the world. Other vendors offered their own versions, and newspapers began moving into the world of digital picture handling.

Digital cameras had been improved but still had a long way to go. AP photographer Ed Reinke used one model at a World Series game, but it had the camera tethered to a portable hard drive unit. They called it portable because you could carry it, but it was hardly something you would want to tote around very much.

To add to the problem, the responsiveness of the camera left something to be desired, too. Reinke practically had to push the shutter button on the camera as a runner rounded third base, if he wanted to get any possible play at home plate. But, when he had something, it was on the wire several minutes ahead of film shot on the same play.

The idea was good. It was the execution that was lacking.

Jump forward to the mid-1990s. Kodak, traditionally linked with film photography, partnered with the AP to introduce a professional digital camera. The camera did have limitations, again traceable to expense and quality concerns, but for the first time photographers could work with equipment that was quite similar to their traditional film cameras.

No longer was a hard-drive side pack needed. The new cameras used internal storage on small disks, and, in conjunction with the faster, lighter laptop computers just coming on the market, photographers truly could make pictures and transmit them almost instantly from a news scene or sports event. Quality was beginning to improve, too.

As the new millennium dawned, the latest generation of digital still cameras came into the marketplace. Much less expensive, with quality that's close to what can be achieved on film, the new cameras allowed newspapers to fully move into the digital age.

"The rate by which news organizations, both print and on-line divisions, have transitioned from traditional wet processing to digital processing has accelerated greatly in the last two years and will continue to accelerate with the new cameras that are coming into the marketplace," says Kenny Irby, the visual journalism group leader at the Poynter Institute.

Those new cameras with their ease of handling and better quality are hitting at a time when newsrooms are ready to make the change. "In terms of image quality for newspaper and magazine and web production," Irby says, "the image quality is solid enough, has enough resolution that people are comfortable with it."

Photographers learn new lessons every day

Hal Buell: "Learn your tools and learn how they work. And that includes writing, which is grammar and structure and narrative. So when the time comes and the opportunity presents itself to do the meaningful story, you can think about and concentrate more on the content. The tools can work for you almost unattended. If you look at the history of journalism, the dynamic between technology and journalism is staggering. Pictures didn't mean anything until the technology came along for books, which allowed the pictures to be shown in them. You have to know the technology to get the picture out there. Don't get to the content before you are ready. Just as the artist has to know that blue and yellow makes green, and how something looks on a particular kind of canvas, the photographer and writer have to know their tools, too."

Elise Amendola: "Never be satisfied. Keep looking, keep shooting. Don't think that you've gotten the picture. Keep working it until the end. You have to be awake and alert to it."

That hasn't always been true. But Irby wonders if the concerns came more from the industry itself than from the readers.

"It had never really been an issue that viewers had rejected the quality of the image," he says. "It has been the issue of the journalist trying to maintain the high quality standards that they have set for themselves."

AP photographer David Longstreath knows how the digital camera has made it easier for him to cover events in some of the farthest corners of the world. And, he has heard discussions on perceived quality problems. He's not convinced that any of those concerns can match up to the new kind of news coverage that has been the product of the technology.

"We are not in the business to make pictures to hang on the wall," Longstreath says. "We are in the business to get pictures in newspapers and magazines and on the Web." He says the proof is in the positive comments of editors as they receive pictures faster than ever before. "They have simply looked at the images and they were strong. The fact that they were digital wasn't an issue."

Now, journalists are comfortable enough with the technology that they can get back to thinking about content rather than quality or technology.

Toren Beasley, the photo chief of the Newhouse News Service, thinks there is a danger of technology, rather than content, being the centerpoint.

Being able to work in remote areas with all of the conveniences of virtually instant editing and feedback are a couple of the reasons David Longstreath fully integrates the digital camera into his everyday work including this portrait of a Long Neck woman, part of a tribe found near the Cambodian-Thailand border who bind their necks with rings.

"This is not about photography," he says. "It may be about different ways to capture images and meet deadlines, but it is not about photography. It is about meeting deadlines, about the speed of bringing an image from one place to another so it can get into the newspaper."

But, it is not about communicating, Beasley says, and that is what journalists should be concerned about.

Irby thinks the time may be right to shift discussions from technical concerns to ways to communicate better.

"Based on not only my travels and work in newsrooms, but also my recent Super Bowl experience," says Irby, "we have witnessed that there is a point where photographers and photo editors are comfortable enough with the technology that they can start focusing on the storytelling more."

The cost of the technology used to be the big drawback. Not so, any more. Digital cameras and computers are half what they cost just a few years ago.

"The real impediment to the full utilization of the digital camera is not expense anymore," Irby says. "It has been clearly demonstrated by many publications around the world that the return on investment on the digital camera has been a positive bene-

The responsiveness of the newest generation of digital cameras allowed AP photographer Mike Conroy to shoot a sequence of Kevin Dyson of the Tennessee Titans diving for the end zone in vain as time ran out in the 2000 Super Bowl.

fit, an advantageous one for news organizations when you consider over time the expenses that are eliminated in terms of film, processing, silver recovery. When you think of all of the environmental protection issues and OSHA rulings, and things like that, there are major benefits."

Instead, it appears the one thing that will keep the cameras from being fully integrated into newspapers' newsgathering operations is training.

Previously, new photography techniques and technologies were just extensions of older, accepted routines. A new lens, a new camera with some extra capabilities, maybe a new enlarger or darkroom device.

But the new digital cameras, the software and computers to support them, and the integration with newsroom systems is a new world.

"There is a reasonable amount of training and reorientation that photographers and photo editors need to go through to understand how to really operate effectively in a digital environment," Irby says. "That is

The emergence of digital photography has had an incredible impact on how photographers work. In 1938, AP photographer Bill Allen had to curl up in the trunk of his car to soup film at the scene of a coal mine explosion (above, left), while Elise Amendola was able to shoot pictures and transmit them from topside ten miles at sea using a laptop linked to a cell phone on the 1997 voyage of Old Ironsides (above). In 1936, technical wizard Harold Carlson needed all kinds of equipment and even car batteries for his setup at the Kentucky Derby (above, right).

something that certainly can be learned without a lot of instruction. But it is really problematic when you go that route."

Instead, Irby says, the newspapers that have made a successful switch most easily have done it with a solid plan for training.

At the 1992 Republican National Convention a photo editor under the camera platform was able to operate a remote camera and send pictures almost instantly as the proceedings took place.

gives the photographer to cover an event and quickly handle those pictures. That's key in a deadline situation.

"If you have a digital camera," she says, "and a laptop computer and a cell phone and an AC-DC converter for your car, you can go anywhere and cover anything and send a picture to anybody without having to knock on the door or build a darkroom or go back home to do it in your basement."

"It makes you fast and efficient and self-reliant," she says.

Longstreath is another who made the conversion early on. And, three

They also have had a timetable that allowed the technology to be accepted into the newsroom with minimal disruptions.

One of the photographers who has made the switchover to digital photography is Amy Sancetta of the AP. She sounds like she is sold on it.

"Shooting with a digital camera makes you, as a photojournalist, completely independent," she says. "You don't need a darkroom. You don't even need electricity."

Sancetta thinks the selling point for digital photography is the independence it

months after getting his camera and a couple of days of training, Longstreath found himself running down the street toward the smoking remains of the Oklahoma City federal building with his one digital camera and two disks in hand.

He made his pictures and then got to a phone to transmit a lot faster than anyone would have expected if had he been shooting film. "Some people may have been hesitant to use the equipment," Longstreath says. "But a lot of people said, 'It worked there. It will work anywhere.'"

"It has completely changed the way we cover news," he says. "Now we can file right from the site. It has allowed us to stay longer, to provide a better mixture of images. It gives you the freedom to stay

---

First camera?

Cliff Schiappa: "My father's Kodak Retina Reflex Three, a hand-me-down."

Mike Morris: "It was a Kodak box camera, black, with the little mechanical shutter. My grandmother gave it to me in junior high school."

Michel DuCille: A Yashica GN. DuCille's camera didn't allow him to set shutter speeds, only the aperture. Had symbols ("zigzag for flash, sun for outside") to set exposures.

Bob Lynn: Got his first, an Ansco box camera, as he was shipping out for Europe in the Army. His father bought it for him as a birthday present.

---

with a story where in the past you had to go and hunt down a darkroom. I often think of all of the times we were on our hands and knees in a toilet trying to soup film. It has made life easier for me."

Irby agrees with those assessments. "The tremendous asset," he says, "that the digital camera brings in terms of competitiveness and covering late deadlines and breaking news issues is what every news organiza-

tion needs to be considering."

Charles Arbogast is an AP photographer based in Trenton, N.J. For several months in 2000, Arbogast was assigned to the presidential campaign of Bill Bradley. He saw another aspect of the digital world.

Often Arbogast would cover an appearance by Bradley, then file the pictures by cell phone from his laptop in the photo van while the candidate's caravan headed to the next stop.

Those pictures would be transmitted by the AP to its members and clients and soon Bradley's campaign staff would be seeing them, too.

"The campaigns were watching Yahoo and Excite all the time," Arbogast says, "because moments after I was transmitting a photo, Internet sites were posting them. I saw printouts of my photos, and other photographers', posted on the campaign office walls. Due to the explosion of photography on the Web, they were able to comment in real time."

Freelance photographer Ami Vitale says the Internet has given her an easy way to do research on her stories and to contact potential clients. "I never would have been able to do this work without the technology that exists today," she says. "I try to do as much research as I can before I go anywhere. And, I try to make connections with people by Internet."

It also allows her to seek markets for her work. "I find that 90 percent of my time is spent on the Internet pitching stories," she says.

For those photographers who don't have digital cameras, there is a definite competitive disadvantage, but all is not lost. Lightweight, portable film scanners, linked to a laptop, give all photographers mobility.

Though she lacks a digital camera, Vitale covers stories in Africa and Eastern Europe for a variety of clients, mostly in the United States. The technology of laptops, scanners and widespread Internet access have made it possible for her to seek out stories without being as concerned about the logistics as she would have been ten years ago.

While she sometimes thinks a digital camera would make her more competitive, she is able to get her pictures out from some fairly out-of-the-way places. "There are one-hour places [for film processing] in the most obscure places," she says. "This has allowed me to compete."

She gets her film processed, then scans the images on her laptop and transmits them via e-mail to her clients. With many clients in the United States, the six- to seven-hour time difference helps some, too.

Vitale does work against the clock, though, in terms of competing with other photographers. In spot news situations such as her recent assignments in Kosovo and Albania, she says she is "usually trying to find a nice moment quickly." But it is difficult "to stay and work a situation to its full potential, because I have to make that deadline."

It doesn't help, she says, that she also has to "try and keep up with the photographers who have digital cameras. If I continue working in spot-news situations, I will need a digital camera," Vitale says. "However, at the moment, I would like to do more magazine-type features which afford me more time," and the chance to put more thinking into her photography.

After all, she says, photography is the name of the game.

Although the explosion of Web sites has meant more outlets for photographs, Vitale says you still need to have the content to be successful.

"It is great having this explosion of sites," she says. "But I think the principles are the same. People are looking for strong images and the bottom line is that you have to come back with a good story and good images. If I shoot something and come back with weak work, whether there are five outlets or 500, I will still have a difficult time selling it."

Sancetta wonders if something has been

> "I think the principles are the same. People are looking for strong images and the bottom line is that you have to come back with a good story and good images. If I shoot something and come back with weak work, whether there are five outlets or 500, I will still have a difficult time selling it."
> — Ami Vitale

Going digital

When digital cameras first appeared, quality was marginal but being able to more quickly move a picture in a deadline situation made that acceptable. Now, photographers use digital cameras in all kinds of situations and there is no downside, only the upside of quicker handling and the savings on continuing costs of film and chemicals.

There don't have to be any apologies or excuses anymore. Photographers are quickly switching to the new technology pushed by budget consideration and operational needs alike.

Here is a gallery of digital images showing the wide range -- David Longstreath's misty river in Vietnam for a travel piece (right), Eric Draper's picture of actor Roberto Benigni celebrating his 1999 Oscar (below), Ed Reinke's picture shot in extremely low light of a Florida player in the locker room after losing the national college basketball title in 2000 (lower right).

Eric Draper photographed the pope in St. Louis (below), Al Behrman used a digital camera for a remote at the Kentucky Derby (right) and had his pictures ready a half-hour sooner than on film, and Amy Sancetta covered the hard news and softer features (bottom) of the 2000 presidential campaign.

lost in this move to the new technology of pictures handled on computer screens. The new generation of photographers, she says, won't know the joy of seeing a print come up in the tray in front of them. They also won't experience the adrenaline rush of racing back to the darkroom to process film on deadline.

"I think we are at a turning point," she says. "When I was a young photographer at the *Columbus Dispatch,* the older photographers at the paper would give us a bad time about going to Ohio State football games with our motor-driven 35 mm cameras." There's that technology argument on a different scale.

"In a good-natured way, they would give us a hard time about how many frames we would shoot, and they would tell us about how they would go to a game with a 4x5 camera with four holders, eight pictures. They would cover a whole game with only eight shots. They said they always came back with the right picture. We would come back with eight rolls of film from the game," she says.

Sancetta isn't sure whether she would have been a better photographer had she had to face those limitations. And, the same kind of argument fits in today's transition to digital photography.

"What it has done is free the photographers to think about pictures rather than the technical aspect," says AP photo editor Bob Daugherty. But, he warns, "Sometimes that freedom is squandered. People go out and bring back a disk with a hundred images, just because the capability is there."

The darkroom experience, Sancetta says, is good training for young photographers because it gives them a better understanding of light and how it works. That is probably what will be missed the most -- the knowledge of how light works is key to any kind of photography, film or digital, she says.

"It is too bad they are going to miss out on the printing because it makes you understand light and contrast, all things that are going to help you when you are composing in the camera," she says. "But I don't know that they'll miss it, because they've never done it."

Today's photographers, who have made the transition from film to digital, could face an even bigger hurdle as the next transition may be from still to video.

Rather than a mere change in equipment, this will be a change in the format the photographer works in and the kind of information that is to be gathered.

The concept of a storyteller who will use still images, video or moving images, and sound is only a few years old, and not particularly widespread in its application, but it is certainly on the minds of a lot of people in journalism.

Newspapers and broadcast outlets with Web sites have a need for more content. Dot-coms are springing up every day. They all need more content.

And, as mergers bring together media companies that have been based in print and others that have been based in broadcast, along with a mix of the new media of the Internet, a different kind of journalist may be in the offing.

Irby sees it happening in this decade in a

limited manner. "I think in the next ten years what we will see is an era where more photographers will be specialized photographers on staffs," he says. Irby thinks just as some newspapers have photographers who specialize in fashion or sports, some may begin to seek photographers who are trained and talented multimedia photographers.

Irby says a lot of people are talking about it and trying to decide how to position themselves, much as they did fifteen years ago in discussions about the future of digital still photography.

"It is a buzz," he says. "I think every photo manager has thought about this or is strongly considering how do you get into that arena much like fifteen years ago when everyone was figuring out how do I get into the digital camera craze. I like the fact the photojournalism managers and organizations are looking ahead, which is a perspective that newspapers have not historically had."

Most agree it will take a versatile photographer to juggle the demands of audio, video and still resources.

Bob Lynn, now a consultant after a career as a director of photography at newspapers in Charleston, W.Va., and Norfolk, Va., has to chuckle a little when he hears talk of "the ultimate storyteller."

Years ago, while working at the *Los Angeles Times* and then later for a short time at *The Cincinnati Enquirer,* Lynn was that era's version of a multimedia journalist. He wrote stories and shot the pictures to go with those stories.

And he knows how hard it is to simultaneously pursue more than one journalistic discipline well at the same time. "I loved it, and it was great," he says. "But I couldn't be quite the writer I wanted to be. And, I couldn't be quite the photographer that I had the potential to be."

The *Washington Post's* Michel DuCille thinks there will be people who will attempt to mesh the worlds of video and audio and still photography, but he doubts there will be much success.

"I believe there will be people who will attempt that," DuCille says, "but over the years they will find you cannot serve two masters. You can't straddle the line between being a still photographer and being a videographer. I think each has their own set of mindsets that require different pacing, different timing."

One aspect of the new multimedia journalism is audio. DuCille thinks that will be a tough one. He recently traveled to Sierra Leone on assignment and tried to capture sound to go along with his still images. "I took along a minidisk and it was the

> "I think in the next ten years what we will see is an era where more photographers will be specialized photographers on staffs."
> — Kenny Irby

> Most agree it will take a versatile photographer to juggle the demands of audio, video and still resources.

hardest thing in the world to stop and figure out, 'Where am I going to put the mike?' How do you capture real moments when you've got to be the one that stops to figure where the microphone goes?" he asks.

Beasley doesn't want the technology to water down the communication. "Technology, until it develops to the point where it is used to impart meaning to an image, to bring the reader to another place emotionally and intellectually, then it is not about the craft. Photography is about communication," he says.

Larry Nighswander of Ohio University's School of Visual Communication is concerned, too. But for a different reason.

"There is no question in my mind," he says, "that there are a lot more storytelling tools available today than there were ten years ago. What I don't think is any more available than ten years ago is the number of people who are excellent storytellers."

He looks through publications now and thinks that the level of photography is barely acceptable. He has seen little improvement over the years. Shouldn't photographers be paying more attention now than ever to content rather than the mechanics of making the picture?

"It is easier today to make pictures than it was with a Nikon F," he says, "so how

> "There is no question in my mind that there are a lot more storytelling tools available today than there were ten years ago. What I don't think is any more available than ten years ago is the number of people who are excellent storytellers."
>
> —Larry Nighswander

do we think that we are just going to overnight or even in ten years turn out these thoughtful stories?"

"If you simply hand a mediocre photographer a DAT recorder and a digital video camera and a digital camera and send them out, we will probably have mediocre video, mediocre sound and mediocre stills," he says. "So we aren't going to be any better off than before."

Daugherty asks if the equipment itself might cause problems. "You've got more moving parts, more bulk weight, more things to worry about. Getting all of those things working together won't be easy," he says.

Irby thinks any setback in quality or content will be short-lived.

"There is a potential to dilute the quality of storytelling initially when you have a traditional journalist from the legacy era trying to operate in the brave new world," he says. Those traditional journalists may have a difficult time making that transition

"But what we have to understand is that there are students who are coming along in a multimedia world," Irby says, "who've grown up on computers, who've grown up thinking about video and still more seamlessly than a traditional photojournalist."

These young journalists are using the new technology to create important, credible pieces. "You can't poke holes in it, because it is thoughtful and it works," Irby says. "We can't underestimate the ability of the human mind and the possibilities that young people will bring to the table as we continue to grow and develop in this area."

Photographer Jennifer Loomis, who has done prize-winning projects on her own and now works for MSNBC, is one who has been successful at combining eye-catching still images with sound to tell a more complete story. She thinks that is a powerful combination.

When shooting the still photos, Loomis says she is trying to think of layers of information. What is in the foreground? What is in the background? Where is the light? What kind of information can I pack in this picture that is going to inform?

And, she thinks she can do the same thing with audio. "There is excitement to audio," she says, and that excitement enriches the story for the reader or viewer. Like her photos, the audio adds a layer of information.

Loomis admits, though, that this kind of storytelling may not be for everyone. "It seems to me that the still-audio combination catches a different kind of person. You have to sit and concentrate on it," she says. "The audio is an accent adding information."

Many people, particularly younger readers and viewers, don't want to spend that

> Jennifer Loomis is one who has been successful at combining eye-catching still images with sound to tell a more complete story. She thinks that is a powerful combination.

time and, for them, the quick infusion of information that video brings is the answer. Loomis isn't among them, however. She doesn't even own a TV. "I'm a live video producer here [at MSNBC], but TV makes me tired," she says, laughing. She finds an afternoon listening to NPR is more relaxing.

And, for the skeptics who question whether a photographer can handle the demands of stills, audio and video at the same time, Loomis thinks it is just a matter of paying attention. While there are times when she'll miss a picture because she is handling the sound, she understands the concern but thinks it is worth the gamble. "The audio enriches the project or story on such a deeper level that it is worth it," she says.

It is frustrating when you miss a picture, she says. "But it is a decision I made early on. When you are doing audio, there are certain shots that you are going to be in the wrong place or the light is going to suck. If you are really working and trying to push yourself, you are going to miss some. It is just the circumstances. You just try to minimize those situations."

She is quick to add, however, that if a key picture is in the balance, the photography aspect of her reporting wins. "If I know I am building up to a picture that is interesting to the story, then my approach is that the photo is the main medium," Loomis says.

In the Web world

Still photography, video, audio. All of the elements combined for a new way of storytelling that calls for a new skill – the multimedia news producer.

Courtney O'Neill of MSNBC got her start in college working for a Boston television station where she picked up her video and audio skills. Then, in a stint in the AP's New York photo operation, she learned about still images.

Now, she combines all of those skills each day to put together information for the MSNBC Web site. And, that's a juggling act. O'Neill monitors breaking news from parent NBC and also watches other assets, as they are called in the multimedia world, such as the 300 video feeds that come pouring into the site's Secaucus, N.J. headquarters. She also checks with news and still photo feeds from the major agencies and contributing freelancers.

When news breaks, she tries to get audio as quickly as possible, then begins blending the other elements as they become available.

"The first layer to a story is an audio report from the scene," O'Neill says.

"Then what we do is to add pictures as they move (from the agencies), then incorporate the stills with video as it arrives and produce a complete package," she says. "Adding a more rich dimension to the storytelling is what the web is there for."

O'Neill says the site's appetite for images and sound is enormous. "We use between 150 and 200 pictures a day," she says. And, while everyone is marveling at how much quicker digital photography is moving now than the old film methods of before, O'Neill says the Web doesn't think that is fast enough. "As soon as the story moves, we want to be positioning pictures," she says.

"The site is an ever-evolving newspaper," O'Neill says. "A newspaper on the fly but with depth. We have a lot of interactive elements that draw people in and give them more information."

"We want to make sure our site is as current as the news," she says. "It isn't like a newspaper where they pick the one or two best pictures of the day. That half-hour, that fifteen minutes, that is what we are going for."

To handle all of that, a hybrid has sprung up – juggler, photo editor, video producer, audio technician and writer. A brave new world of storytelling for the journalist.

Loomis agrees with others that the important thing is the information you are giving the reader or viewer, regardless of the medium. She specializes in essays that have a social message, essays like her prize-winning look at aging in Japan, When Flowers Fall. They are on the cutting edge, with combined elements of still photography, audio and a written story, but the overall content is what is important.

"I believe people want to care," Loomis says. "They want to be drawn into something. You just have to give them the content."

Rob Kozloff, who has been a picture editor for the AP and the *Detroit Free Press,* thinks we'll go through the same kinds of discussions on quality that we did during other transitions in photography.

"People will fight it," he says. "Just like the transition from 4x5 to 2-1/4, then to 35 mm. Then, going all color. But eventually the discussions end. We just have to move with this."

Kozloff says he personally wonders what it will be like when you get your news and information exclusively on a screen rather

> "People will fight it. Just like the transition from 4x5 to 2-1/4, then to 35 mm. Then, going all color. But eventually the discussions end. We just have to move with this."
> — Rob Kozloff

than in a printed newspaper. "A lot of us love to sit down with the paper," he says. "I would just as soon not read it on a screen. But, how many more years will you be able to do this?"

AP photographer Elise Amendola thinks it is a simple case of the still image being the most powerful way to tell a story.

At the end of the day, regardless of the kind of technology that has been used to capture an image, she says, "it better be able to stand up on its own. It is not supported by all the other sensory input."

"I think the still image will always be more powerful for that reason," she says. "Video is diluted with sound and motion. There is nothing more powerful than a well-timed moment that cuts to the heart and tells the story."

Or, as AP photo editor Horst Faas puts it, "The story may have a thousand words, but you will look at that one best picture over and over again. Studying it from different angles. The one best that stands for it all."

Contributors

The following journalists and educators are quoted or have photographs in this book:

Amendola, Elise - The Associated Press, Boston

Anderson, Juana - *The Washington Post*

Applewhite, J. Scott - The Associated Press, Washington

Arbogast, Charles Rex - The Associated Press, Trenton

Baumann, J. Bruce - *The Courier and Press*, Evansville, Ind.

Beasley, Toren - Newhouse News Service, Washington

Becker, Murray - The Associated Press

Behrman, Al - The Associated Press, Cincinnati

Biever, John - Sports Illustrated magazine, Milwaukee

Binks, Porter - Sports Illustrated magazine, New York

Bouju, Jean-Marc - freelance, Nairobi

Buell, Harold G. - The Associated Press, New York

Bukaty, Robert - The Associated Press, Portland, Maine

Burrows, Alex - *The Virginian-Pilot*, Norfolk

Cabluck, Harry - The Associated Press, Austin

Carter, J. Pat - The Associated Press, Oklahoma City

Carter, Mary Ann - freelance, Indianapolis

Clarkson, Rich - Rich Clarkson & Associates, Denver

Conroy, Mike - The Associated Press, Indianapolis

Counts, Wyatt - freelance, New York

Daugherty, Bob - The Associated Press, Washington

Delay, Jerome - The Associated Press, Paris

Diaz, Alan - The Associated Press, Miami

Draper, Eric - The Associated Press, Albuquerque

DuCille, Michel - *The Washington Post*

Duncan, Mark - The Associated Press, Cleveland

Endlicher, Diether - The Associated Press, Munich

Faas, Horst - The Associated Press, London

Friedman, Rick - freelance, Boston

Gaps, John III - *The Des Moines Register*

Gash, Morry - The Associated Press, Milwaukee

Gay, Eric - The Associated Press, San Antonio

Grant, Alistair - freelance, London

Guttenfelder, David - The Associated Press, Tokyo

Hulshizer, Dan - The Associated Press, Trenton

Humphrey, Mark - The Associated Press, Nashville

Irby, Kenny - The Poynter Institute, St. Petersburg

Keiser, Beth - The Associated Press, New York

Kemper, Gary - Sydney Organizing Committee for the Olympic Games

Kennedy, Rusty - The Associated Press, Philadelphia

Kozloff, Rob - *The Detroit Free-Press*

Lederhandler, Marty - The Associated Press, New York

Lee, Wilfredo - The Associated Press, Miami

Lennihan, Mark - The Associated Press, New York

Longstreath, David - The Associated Press, Bangkok

Loomis, Jennifer - freelance, MSNBC, Seattle

Lynn, Bob - photography/graphics consultant, Charleston, W.Va.

McConnico, John - The Associated Press, New Delhi

Marti, Enric - The Associated Press, Cairo

Martin, David - The Associated Press, Montgomery, Ala.

Mell, Jeanne - *The News-Journal*, Wilmington, Del.

Meyer, Jens - freelance, Hanover, Germany

Mills, Doug - The Associated Press, Washington

Moore, John - The Associated Press, Mexico City

Morse, Michael - Western Kentucky University, Bowling Green

Nash, Michael - The Associated Press

Nighswander, Larry - Ohio University School of Visual Communication, Athens

Nighswander, Marcy - Ohio University School of Visual Communication, Athens

O'Neill, Coutney - MSNBC, New York

Phillip, David - The Associated Press, Houston

Pizac, Doug - The Associated Press, Salt Lake City

Puskar, Gene - The Associated Press, Pittsburgh

Ragan, Susan - The Associated Press, San Francisco

Rauch, Laura - The Associated Press, Las Vegas

Reinke, Ed - The Associated Press, Louisville

Risberg, Eric - The Associated Press, San Francisco

Sakuma, Paul - The Associated Press, San Francisco

Sancetta, Amy - The Associated Press, Chagrin Falls, Ohio

Sancya, Paul - The Associated Press, Detroit

Savoia, Stephan - The Associated Press, Boston

Schiappa, Cliff - The Associated Press, Kansas City

Stewart, Gary - rancher, Seattle

Sullivan, Pat - The Associated Press, Houston

Terrill, Mark - The Associated Press, Los Angeles

Vitale, Ami - freelance, Washington

Vranic, Dusan - The Associated Press, Brussels

Widman, George - The Associated Press, Philadelphia

Zelevansky, Jeff - freelance, New York